An
American
Vision

Wendy A. Cooper

*with the assistance of Tara L. Gleason and Katharine A. John*

# An American Vision

*Henry Francis du Pont's*

# Winterthur Museum

National Gallery of Art, Washington

Winterthur Museum, Garden & Library, Delaware

The exhibition is made possible by Louisa and Robert Duemling.

In celebration of our 200th anniversary, DuPont is proud to sponsor this exhibition.

The exhibition is organized by Winterthur and the National Gallery of Art, Washington

**Exhibition Dates**
5 May – 6 October 2002
National Gallery of Art, Washington

*The exhibition catalogue is made possible by grants from Linda H. Kaufman and the Kaufman Americana Foundation in memory of George M. Kaufman; The Alexandria Association; and The Washington Decorative Arts Forum.*

Produced by the Editors Office, National Gallery of Art

Judy Metro, Editor-in-Chief
Julie Warnement, Editor
Margaret Bauer, Designer

Special photography by Gavin Ashworth

Typeset in Adobe Caslon, Requiem Display, and FF Fago Condensed by the National Gallery of Art and printed on Parilux Matt 150 gsm by Balding + Mansell, Norwich, England

**Library of Congress Cataloguing-in-Publication Data** | Cooper, Wendy A. An American vision: Henry Francis du Pont's Winterthur Museum / Wendy A. Cooper with the assistance of Tara L. Gleason and Katharine A. John.
p. cm.
Catalog of an exhibition organized by the Winterthur Museum and the National Gallery of Art, which was on display at the Gallery in Washington, D.C., May 5 – Oct. 6, 2002.
Includes bibliographical references and index.

ISBN 0-85331-859-x (cloth)
ISBN 0-89468-294-6 (paper)

1. Decorative arts – United States – Exhibitions. 2. Decorative arts – Delaware – Winterthur – Exhibitions. 3. Henry Francis du Pont Winterthur Museum – Exhibitions. I. Gleason, Tara Louise. II. John, Katharine A. III. Henry Francis du Pont Winterthur Museum. IV. National Gallery of Art (U.S.) V. Title.

NK805.C678 2002
745′.0973′0747511 – dc21
2002022114

Clothbound edition first published in 2002 by the National Gallery of Art and Winterthur in association with Lund Humphries, Gower House, Croft Road, Aldershot, Hampshire GU11 3HR, UK, and 131 Main Street, Burlington, Vermont 05401. Lund Humphries is part of Ashgate Publishing.

*www.lundhumphries.com*

**British Library Cataloguing-in-Publication Data** | A catalogue record for this book is available from the British Library

**Illustrations**
Front cover: (top) detail of palampore, India, 1690–1720; (bottom) Du Pont Dining Room, north wall, sideboard, New York, 1795–1805; tankards, Paul Revere, Boston, 1772; and urn-shaped knife boxes, England, 1790–1800; (flap) box, Berks or Northampton County, Pennsylvania, 1770–1800

Back cover: (right) Montmorenci Staircase, removed from an 1822 house in Shocco Springs, North Carolina, and adapted by Thomas T. Waterman and du Pont for Winterthur; (top left) covered cup, Jurian Blanck Jr., New York, about 1690; (bottom left) detail of quilt, eastern United States, 1795–1825; (flap, paper edition) detail of *Washington at Verplanck's Point*, John Trumbull, New York, 1790

Frontispiece: Winterthur, as Henry Francis du Pont knew it during his youth (1880s–1890s). About 1884, his father added a steeply pitched slate roof, dormers, and tall brick chimneys to the original 1839 structure.

Page 8: Du Pont's desk, Cecil Bedroom. H. F. chose this elegant Queen Anne New Hampshire desk and Boston side chair for use in his own bedroom.

Page 197: Winterthur's azalea woods, spring. This harmony of pinks and greens blends into the broader pastoral vista of the vast country estate.

Pages 206–207: Winterthur Museum today.

Page 215: Reverse-painted glass (detail), ladies desk (chapter 5, fig. 4)

# Contents

**Foreword**

Earl A. Powell III
*Director, National Gallery of Art*

Leslie Greene Bowman
*Director, Winterthur Museum, Garden & Library*

In this year when we truly have reason to cherish our American values and heritage, the National Gallery of Art is proud to supplement its outstanding collections of American art with an exhibition of superb American decorative arts from Winterthur—the greatest such collection in the nation. Nowhere has a museum preserved more beautifully and comprehensively the artistic evidence of our ancestors' lives. This volume, in addition to the exhibition that it accompanies, offers insights into Winterthur's unique history and connection with the du Pont family, profiles Henry Francis du Pont's favorite subcollections, and presents a compelling tribute to American artistry and craftsmanship.

Never before has Winterthur allowed a major exhibition of its world-class collection to travel. This special project celebrates Winterthur's fiftieth anniversary as a public institution as well as its critical role in preserving our country's legacy in the decorative arts. It is fitting that such an exhibition should occur in the nation's capital at the National Gallery of Art.

We are grateful to all who have made this project such a pleasure for staff, visitors, and readers alike. The fruits of their efforts are readily seen. To the dedicated curator of the exhibition and author of this publication, Wendy A. Cooper, the Lois F. and Henry S. McNeil Senior Curator of Furniture at Winterthur, we extend our deepest appreciation. Her knowledge, expertise, and insights have contributed immeasurably to the experience that awaits one and all.

We owe particular thanks to Louisa and Robert Duemling and to the DuPont Company, whose generous support has made *An American Vision* possible. Henry Francis du Pont's great-grandfather founded the DuPont Company in 1802. DuPont has been a steadfast supporter of Winterthur throughout its fifty years, and in this project it honors Winterthur's anniversary and its own bicentennial. We are grateful to Chad Holliday, chairman and chief executive officer, for recognizing in this project a worthy tribute to an extraordinary cultural legacy and a great global corporation with its roots in America. This publication benefited from the support of the Kaufman Americana Foundation, The Alexandria Association, and The Washington Decorative Arts Forum. We are grateful to Linda H. Kaufman and the late George M. Kaufman for their steadfast support of American decorative arts.

**Acknowledgments**

Wendy A. Cooper
*Lois F. and Henry S. McNeil Senior Curator*
*of Furniture at Winterthur*

Major presentations—whether they take the form of exhibitions or publications—are the result of both vision and persistence. Had it not been for both of these qualities on the part of numerous dedicated and creative people, this effort could not have come to fruition. First and foremost I want to commend the vision of both Leslie Greene Bowman, director, Winterthur Museum, Garden & Library, and Earl A. Powell III, director, National Gallery of Art. Together their enthusiasm and determination moved this effort forward in this very special fiftieth anniversary year for Winterthur. I thank them for the opportunity and privilege of curating this exhibition and authoring its publication.

In every respect this project has been a team effort, with collegial professionals from both institutions working together for a stunning result. The efforts of several chief officers have been critical: I thank Winterthur's Alex Sydnor and the Gallery's Ruth Anderson Coggeshall, Christine Myers, and Deborah Ziska. From the start, the project has benefited from the enthusiastic leadership of Patricia Halfpenny, Winterthur's director of collections. The contributions from each of Winterthur's specialist curators have been invaluable: Linda Eaton, textiles and needlework, Donald F. Fennimore, metalwork, Leslie Grigsby, ceramics and glass, and Anne Verplanck, paintings, prints, and drawings. I thank them all not only for their lead in the selection of objects, but also for their research assistance, reading and critique of the text, and unending moral support. Additionally, I want to thank Ronald Fuchs, assistant curator, and Neville Thompson, senior librarian, for their assistance with research details.

As the exhibition began to take shape, National Gallery of Art colleagues were indefatigable in their appetite for American decorative arts. The selection was honed and the installation brilliantly designed by Mark Leithauser, senior curator, chief of design, with guidance and support from D. Dodge Thompson, chief of exhibitions, Susan M. Arensberg, head of exhibition programs, and Franklin Kelly, curator of American and British paintings. The resulting presentation at the Gallery is extraordinary, representing one more instance of the vision and persistence that have pervaded this project's success.

Objects are obviously the driving force of any exhibition or publication, and the professionals who orchestrate both the proper conservation of them and their safe movement have worked tirelessly to ensure their security and aesthetic presentation. At Winterthur, registrar Grace Eleazer, associate registrar Amy Dowe, and director of conservation Gregory Landrey with focus and dedication have orchestrated their colleagues, as objects have been assessed, conserved, photographed, and ultimately packed and transported. And at the National Gallery, chief registrar Sally Freitag worked with Melissa Stegeman, assistant registrar, and Naomi Remes, exhibition officer. My sincere thanks go to them and their staffs for much that was above and beyond the call, and occasionally in a tight time framework.

For the beauty, balance, and harmony of this publication, I owe the deepest gratitude to those who worked seemingly double time to meet ever-pressing deadlines. Gavin Ashworth's expert and brilliantly produced special photographs have made the design of this work a joy, and his "there's no 'I' in team" attitude made him a delightful colleague. The editors office at the National Gallery has as usual been superb, with editor-in-chief Judy Metro leading the way with constructive critique and direction. The greatest pleasure has been the ultimate birth of this book as the superior editorial skills of Julie Warnement polished my prose, and the keen design talents of Margaret Bauer wove images and words into a visually meaningful whole.

For their organizational skills, research support, and everyday attentiveness to this project, I am indebted to Tara L. Gleason, assistant curator, and Katharine A. John, curatorial assistant. Their enthusiastic spirit and can-do approach to everything not only have made the past year a pleasure, but also have moved this entire project forward with alacrity and professionalism. Finally, I want to add a personal note of thanks to Linda H. Kaufman and the late George M. Kaufman for their financial support as well as for their continuous interest in and enthusiasm for this project.

# Winterthur: An American Country Estate

*Leslie Greene Bowman*

WINTERTHUR IS A PLACE OF EXCELLENCE and inspiration. Its museum and garden are crowning achievements in their respective fields, and each is a tour de force of presentation. The Winterthur library is equally noteworthy as the finest resource of its kind. But Winterthur is more than a great museum of American decorative arts, a breathtaking woodland garden, and an outstanding research library. Winterthur is blessed among cultural institutions, for it occupies an enviable site of nearly 1,000 acres in the luxuriant Brandywine Valley. Although today this estate is centered in the most populated corridor of the United States, visitors may still experience the excitement of young Ruth Ellen du Pont's arrival at her weekend home. "Driving from the railroad station we would soon reach real country on the other side of the Gatehouse—owl country, fox country—and would speed down the winding mile-long driveway through the enormous woods and up the hill to the house." Today it is the museum and no longer Ruth's bedroom that looks "down on a meadow...and the Clenny Run stream, whose banks in late spring were crowded with mint, buttercups, and forget-me-nots." [1]

Winterthur remains at heart a great country estate, still home to owls and foxes. At its height Winterthur comprised 2,600 acres and housed or employed more than 250 people. It still retains its picturesque vistas and stately country house demeanor. Great champion trees surround the mansion and shade the 66-acre English "wild" garden, [2] which is rimmed by parks, pastures, and woodlands. Former estate buildings still enliven the landscape—farmhouses, springhouses, train station, barns, and herdsmen's cottages.

14

Winterthur (fig. 1) is the result of one man's passion and his vision to transform his ancestral home into a country estate with cultural distinctions comparable to those of similar sites in Europe. A visit to Winterthur is akin to visiting a great country house such as Chatsworth or Blenheim Palace: a superlative collection, tastefully and sensitively installed throughout the mansion, a house surrounded by a stunning garden, and the whole in a picturesque, bucolic setting. Upon her first visit to Winterthur in 1961, Jacqueline Kennedy exclaimed, "I just can't believe it was possible for anyone to ever do such a thing Mr. du Pont, you now have me in such a state of awe and reverence I may never be able to write you again! I now have an ambition for our old age—for us to be gatekeepers at Winterthur."[3] Yet for a man considered the greatest collector of his generation, perhaps it was not so unbelievable.[4]

Born at Winterthur in 1880, Henry Francis du Pont, also known as H. F. or Harry, was the third generation of du Ponts to dwell on the grounds. His great-grandfather, Eleuthère Irénée du Pont de Nemours (1771–1834), was the French-born founder of the gunpowder firm that would become the DuPont Company. Winterthur was originally part of E. I. du Pont's estate, a 445-acre parcel that was purchased by his business partner and son-in-law, James Antoine Bidermann, and his daughter, Evelina, in 1837. Bidermann, the son of a Swiss investor in the company, and Evelina named their farm Winterthur for his ancestral home, a Swiss town northeast of Zurich. The next inhabitant was Evelina's nephew, Col. Henry Algernon du Pont (Henry Francis' father), who expanded the acreage considerably. When H. F. inherited Winterthur in 1927, it was a sprawling estate of 2,400 acres.

**1** | Winterthur today | The original Winterthur house built by the Bidermanns, then enlarged by H. F. du Pont's father, is now part of the large wing on the left. To the right is the massive addition, added to the back of the house by H. F. With that expansion, he created a new entrance with the pedimented doorway (lower right) and transformed the former front portico into a conservatory.

**2** | *Henry Francis du Pont,* Ellen Emmet Rand, New York, 1914 | Although only thirty-four when this portrait was painted, du Pont had already managed the estate's gardens and grounds for eight years. In 1914, the same year Rand completed this portrait, du Pont assumed total responsibility for Winterthur, inside and out.

The house of Harry's childhood was one-third the size it is today. The formal interiors were laden with imported European textiles and furniture, in keeping with prevailing taste. French was spoken in the home, and Harry learned English as a second language. His father was formal and demanding, once scolding the boy, "You must be worthy of the name you bear!"[5] H.F. was an unmotivated student, both at Groton and Harvard, until he discovered horticulture courses at Harvard's Bussey Institution. He intended to pursue graduate studies in horticulture and agriculture, but his plans were curtailed by his mother's death in 1902. Harry completed his undergraduate degree and returned to Winterthur to manage his father's household in 1903.

The colonel was just completing an expansion and redecoration of the house, aided throughout by his son, who revealed a penchant for design. Harry assumed supervision of the decorating and plunged happily into the details of entertaining and servants' livery. He continued to study gardens during trips abroad and sent thousands of plants home for his revisions to the Winterthur garden. His father, shortly after winning a seat in the United States Senate in 1906, handed over management of the garden and grounds to Harry. In 1914 the colonel bestowed on his son full management of the entire estate, including the considerable agricultural enterprises of the Winterthur Farms. Harry (fig. 2) set about improving the Holstein-Friesian breed of dairy cattle, ultimately creating one of the finest dairy herds in America. He also began redesigning the Winterthur garden with the help of his schoolmate, landscape architect Marian Cruger Coffin.

In 1916, Henry Francis du Pont married Ruth Wales (1889–1967), a society beauty from Hyde Park, New York. The couple lived at Winterthur for awhile, but Ruth found her father-in-law intractable and yearned for a home away from Delaware. They kept an apartment on Park Avenue and in 1924 purchased land in Southampton, Long Island, where they had repeatedly spent summers. They determined to build, as Harry described it, an "American house." Only the previous year H.F. du Pont had discovered the appeal of American antiques and architecture. He later wrote:

*The house at Winterthur, Delaware, my family's home where I was brought up, was furnished with miscellaneous foreign and American Empire pieces, predominantly of veneered mahogany, and these to me had seemed heavy and often lacking in grace. A visit to Mrs. Watson Webb's house in Shelburne, Vermont, in 1923, was therefore a revelation. This was the first early all American interior I had ever seen and it captivated me. I still remember in detail the contrasting colours there of pink Staffordshire against a lovely pine dresser.[6]*

**3** | Library, Chestertown House | Du Pont's dress rehearsal for furnishing a house with antiques occurred when the young couple built their seaside retreat in Southampton, Long Island. Here H. F. developed his own personal style, which he expressed more fully at Winterthur after he inherited it in 1927.

In a later version of the same manuscript, H. F. continued, "Seeing Harry Sleeper's house at Gloucester, Massachusetts, a few days later made me decide to build an American house at Southhampton."[7] The visit to Sleeper's home, Beauport, "crystallized my desire to start collecting Americana on my own. In retrospect, I realize how important was this particular week in shaping the course of my life."[8]

Henry Davis Sleeper was a well-known Boston decorator and collector. His home was the inspiration for the Southampton house and the Winterthur we know today— rooms of early American architecture decorated with American antiques of similar period and locale. Du Pont sought Sleeper's assistance with the Southampton residence, named Chestertown House for the town in Maryland where some of the interior architecture originated. Chestertown House (fig. 3) was a fifty-room colonial revival residence, "in the style of about 1770," according to du Pont's wishes.[9] It catalyzed collecting instincts latent in Harry since his childhood, when he had collected minerals, birds' eggs, and stamps. Du Pont devoted himself to his new-found passion with zeal and considerable means, purchasing woodwork, antique furnishings, and even authentic hardware and nails. In 1924 he acquired 226 pieces of furniture and countless more glass, ceramic, and metal objects.[10] Thus began Henry Francis du Pont's legendary pursuit of American arts, which continued unabated until his death in 1969. The chapters that follow explore H. F.'s all-consuming appetite for the most beautiful and meaningful material remains of America's past.

Du Pont was part of a rising tide of interest in early American craftsmanship. *The Magazine Antiques* had been founded in 1922. In 1924, the year he began Chestertown House, the American Wing opened at New York's Metropolitan Museum of Art, resplendent with period rooms of early American decorative arts. Two years later, John D. Rockefeller commenced the restoration of Colonial Williamsburg, while Henry Ford founded the Edison Institute in Dearborn, Michigan, and began planning a museum and country village devoted to American history, craftsmanship, and ingenuity.[11]

Chestertown House was completed in the summer of 1926 and drew high praise. A visitor that very year remarked, "The pieces that you have assembled in your rooms are such perfect examples of their periods and are so appropriately installed that all may be studied and enjoyed. No section has been crowded and no discordant note is felt…. The idea of a museum is suppressed absolutely, and yet I know of no institution that contains such specimens of early Americana as your beautiful home holds today."[12]

**4** | Construction of addition, east terrace | In 1928, construction crews began work on a large "American Wing" at Winterthur, which more than doubled the size of the house and provided numerous spaces for the multifaceted collections H. F. had already begun to amass.

Only a few months after the home's completion, Col. Henry Algernon du Pont died, leaving Winterthur to his son. There was no longer any question about what H. F. intended to do with his ancestral home. Chestertown House had been a successful experiment, and du Pont was ready to repeat it on a grander scale. By 1928 he had approved plans and embarked on an enormous addition to Winterthur (fig. 4) that more than doubled the size of the house in order to accommodate his growing collection of architecture, woodwork, and decorative arts. He explained his motives: "After the opening of the American Wing at the Metropolitan Museum in New York in 1924, and another such wing in the Brooklyn Museum…it occurred to me to undertake a similar venture, and I decided to add an 'American Wing' to Winterthur, which I had inherited at about this time."[13] He soon determined that the entire house should reflect his new-found passion.

Du Pont increasingly focused on historical accuracy at Winterthur, in contrast with his decorative approach to Chestertown House. He did not relinquish his insistence on harmonious arrangements, but noted, "I am doing the house archaeologically and correctly."[14] He sought architectural interiors from the original thirteen colonies and installed these settings at Winterthur, which today contains one of the largest collections of American architecture in a single institution. His quest to fill the period rooms resulted in literally thousands of purchases a year, ranging from paintings, furniture, silver, and base metalwork, to Chinese export porcelains, slipware, prints, and glass, all dating between 1640 and 1840.

**5** | High chest, Philadelphia, 1760–1780 | This magnificent high chest became an icon of American decorative arts collecting when du Pont acquired it for $44,000 (an auction record) in 1929 at the sale of Howard Reifsnyder's collection. Probably originally owned in the Turner family, it came into the Van Pelt family through marriage in the nineteenth century and has subsequently been dubbed the Van Pelt high chest.

Du Pont was relentless in his insistence on quality, frequently paying heady five-figure sums for furniture. The Reifsnyder sale in April 1929 was described in *International Studio* as a "battle of collectors [that] will probably never be duplicated in any American salesroom."[15] When it was over, a new record had been established for American furniture: du Pont had outbid William Randolph Hearst for the Van Pelt highboy (fig. 5), a stellar example of the eighteenth-century Philadelphia rococo style. The hammer fell at $44,000, and du Pont's intentions and means resounded throughout the antiques world. Collector Louis Guerineau Myers immediately invited du Pont to join the sponsoring committee for a major exhibition of American decorative arts that he was curating in New York City as a benefit for the Girl Scouts of America. The first exhibition of its kind, the now famous *Girl Scouts Loan Exhibition* opened in the Anderson Art Galleries in the fall of 1929 for two weeks.[16] After only six years of collecting, du Pont was the largest single lender. Myers also relied on him for design assistance, noting, "I am sure it will be a tremendous success if you can produce some of the effects of your own home."[17]

What distinguished du Pont from other collectors was not merely his quest for excellence, nor his ability to pay for it, but his talent for arranging the collection. Influenced by Sleeper's sensitivity to design and color, du Pont developed a keen sense of proportion, composition, and color. He attributed these abilities to his lifelong love of the natural world, stating in his eighties, "I have always loved flowers and had a garden as a child,...and if you have grown up with flowers and really seen them you can't help to have unconsciously absorbed an appreciation of proportion, color, detail, and material."[18] He painstakingly arranged his collection to create a unified room, emphasizing, "It's one of my first principles that if you go into a room, and right away see something, then you must realize that that shouldn't be in the room."[19] The effect that Myers so admired is what has made Winterthur a unique experience (see chapter 3, fig. 16).

When the *Girl Scouts Loan Exhibition* opened, the *New York Herald Tribune* commented on the new character of American collecting:

*America today is a nation of collectors more cosmopolitan than any the world has ever known. Yet in the midst of cosmopolitanism our collectors remain finely national. The most widespread love among them is for the relics of our ancestors. The majority of our collectors want to surround themselves—especially in their country houses, where they have the most leisure—with the furniture of our forebears, the portraits of our early Americans and the china, glass and precious bric-a-brac of those who gave our nation to us. This Americana passion is so widespread at present as to be an epidemic rage.*[20]

6 | Winterthur estate vista | When du Pont inherited Winterthur in 1927, the property comprised 2,400 acres. Although much smaller today, the grounds continue to afford visitors sweeping pastoral views.

For du Pont the epidemic had only begun, and the stock market crash had little effect on his resources. In the next great auction following the Reifsnyder sale (that of Philip Flayderman in January 1930), H. F. bought, for $30,000, the record lot of the sale—a rare, labeled writing desk with exquisite inlay and tambour doors, by the Boston firm of John Seymour and Son. That same month he spent $48,700 on a group of furniture and pewter from Louis Guerineau Myers, including an important group of seating furniture attributed to the New York cabinetmaker Duncan Phyfe and a pier table labeled by the French emigré craftsman Charles-Honoré Lannuier.

Despite his use of pseudonyms and secrecy, du Pont was well known to dealers and fellow collectors, and his activities created some rivalries, or at least perceived ones. Francis P. Garvan was another major lender to the *Girl Scouts Loan Exhibition*. In 1930 he began giving his collection—consisting primarily of great American furniture, paintings, and silver—to Yale University. In 1931 he wrote H. F.:

*Apparently we are the only two purchasers of American antiques left in America, and I am a purchaser only to the most limited extent, and I feel that we are being used to our mutual disinterest…. whenever I want a piece I am threatened with it being sold to Mr. du Pont if I do not pay an extravagant price for it, and undoubtedly the same thing is being said to you.*[21]

In 1932, du Pont was invited to join the Walpole Society, an elite group of museum curators and collectors of American art and antiques. The society visited Winterthur that autumn, just a year after the completion of the huge new wing. If du Pont was anxious about hosting the country's most distinguished experts, he need not have been. Brooklyn Museum governor and noted furniture scholar and author Luke Vincent Lockwood exclaimed, "Imagine a house which records the decorative history of our Country, and that in supreme terms!"[22] Three other members responded to the size and ambiance of Winterthur:

*We have seen restored houses, beautifully done… or new houses…, both unforgettably delightful as homes. Yet never have we seen so many old American rooms under one roof—the number seemed endless and we have serious doubts if any of us saw them all—possibly Mr. du Pont himself may sometimes forget a few of them. Or could we imagine that there could be put into one house so many rooms so different in size, period and character, in such way as to make it livable—to make a home of it. But Mr. du Pont has done it. Here are rooms that welcome the guest, furniture which seems glad to receive him. There is nothing of the museum in the air. We are not among the dead.*[23]

And yet, as early as 1930, du Pont had recorded his interest in founding a museum with his collections. He first considered doing so with Chestertown House, but as he perfected Winterthur, he began moving parts of the Chestertown collection down to Delaware. By 1948 he had determined to turn Winterthur into a museum during his lifetime, so that he could actively shape its future. He built another residence on the estate, hosted the last dinner party in the mansion, and moved his family across the driveway to "the cottage," a fifty-room residence in the Regency style. Winterthur Museum opened to the public in October 1951.

Until his death in 1969, du Pont played an active role at Winterthur. To provide the museum with its first curator, H. F. hired Joseph Downs, the nation's leading authority on American decorative arts and a veteran curator of the American Wing at the Metropolitan Museum of Art. And as Winterthur's first director, H. F. selected Downs' close friend Charles F. Montgomery, a dealer and pewter specialist. H. F. also continued to refine the museum. The bowling alley, squash court, kitchens, and bathrooms were removed to accommodate the expanding collection. A spring garden tour was added in 1952, and new facilities for the museum followed: a visitor center, a library, offices, and a conservation laboratory. In 1952, at Montgomery's urging, du Pont forged a unique relationship between Winterthur and the University of Delaware, pioneering a graduate program for the training of museum curators in American decorative arts. Its success was the model for a second program in art conservation founded in 1974.

In 1961, a young First Lady sought validation and counsel on a controversial project to redecorate the White House. Thirty-one-year-old Jacqueline Kennedy turned to octogenarian Henry Francis du Pont, the nation's premier collector and authority on American antiques, to chair the first Fine Arts Committee for the White House (fig. 7). Her choice of a chairman silenced many critics and buoyed fundraising efforts for the project. Du Pont helped her decline most of the hundreds of gifts from America's attics that were immediately offered. He also advised her on appropriate styles and historical accuracy. Du Pont the decorator is most evident in the Green Room, where he selected the furniture and upholstery, and placed the room's contents. But decorating the White House was not the same as decorating Winterthur, where he wielded absolute control. He wrote disapprovingly of the location of a new loan in 1962:

*I am disturbed to learn [that the] mirror in the Green Room has been replaced by the Chippendale mirror lent by Mt. Vernon. This mirror was in a Philadelphia house in which Washington lived, but never in the White House at any time....No matter how handsome, the mirror is a false note in that room to anyone who knows period furniture.*[24]

**7** | Mrs. John F. Kennedy, Henry Francis du Pont, and Dana Taylor, Winterthur, 8 May 1961 | Jacqueline Kennedy selected du Pont to chair her Fine Arts Committee for the White House. As her advisor, du Pont helped shape the style and ambiance of White House furnishings in a manner that reflected the rich decorative arts history of the early American republic.

**8** | Dressing table, Boston, 1700–1720 | Although du Pont sought to acquire a slate-top William and Mary dressing table, he did not succeed in finding an example during his lifetime. Winterthur acquired this table in 1998, fulfilling one of du Pont's goals for the museum's collection.

The mirror was moved, but Jackie insisted on proceeding with the rose watered-silk wallpaper selected with the French decorator Stéphane Boudin for the Queen's Room, instead of an 1824 French scenic paper favored by du Pont, who conceded graciously. Jackie later deemed him a "national blessing" and offered gratitude for his service in a letter of September 1963:

*Dear Mr. du Pont, don't you know that everything that is lovely in The White House now, is all your contribution; who could possibly have made a greater one? You know, I told you in the very beginning that I never wanted any contribution from you but your heart and your time—and, you have given of those so much more than one ever could have hoped for.*[25]

From the mid-1950s until his death, H. F. made notes for his executors and directors detailing his wishes for museum practices, policies, and acquisitions. He noted his desire "to get, if ever available," a William and Mary slate-top table, "one of the most refined and probably finest of this type New England table."[26] Happily, the museum was able to acquire just such a table in 1998 (fig. 8). Devoted to the same standards of excellence as those established by H. F. du Pont, the curators at Winterthur have continued to add distinguished pieces to the collections. With about 85,000 objects, Winterthur remains the greatest collection of decorative arts made or used in America between settlement and 1860. The addition of a dedicated exhibitions building in 1992 has made the collection more accessible, allowing more display space than was available in the mansion's period rooms.

**9** | Winterthur estate | The ponds, fields, and forests of this great American country estate provide changing seasonal vistas throughout the year as well as numerous habitats for various species of both flora and fauna.

Du Pont was deeply committed to representing all periods and media in his American museum, whose collections today are a tremendous resource of objects that teach the chronology of American stylistic development prior to 1860. Although he succeeded beautifully in putting together a comprehensive collection, there is no doubt that some styles, regions, and ethnic expressions appealed more strongly to his eye than did others. And it is these preferences—his most prized pieces—that we have attempted to present in the pages that follow, with chapters highlighting both specific time periods and themes. In making our selection (a difficult prospect without H. F.'s direct guidance), we have followed the same principles that du Pont himself employed: rarity, beauty, historical association, and provenance.

Du Pont had a grand design and vision for Winterthur. For more than forty years he had integrated his masterpieces in room settings, his rooms with the colors of the garden outside, his garden with the surrounding parks and woodlands—the whole was a great country estate (figs. 6, 9). And du Pont was the consummate country gentleman. While nurturing the museum, he never neglected his two other passions—his garden and his dairy herd. Each in its realm attained a significance equal to that of the museum. And yet, he foresaw that Winterthur's size and breadth were not sustainable after his death. Therefore, he reduced the estate to just under 1,000 acres, carefully creating a perimeter greensward to protect core areas. He also directed that the herd be sold if a university agriculture school could not assume its management.

In 1961, du Pont told his long-range planning consultants:

*I sincerely hope that the Museum will be a continuing source of inspiration and education for all time, and that the gardens and grounds will themselves be a country place museum where visitors may enjoy as I have, not only the flowers, trees, and shrubs, but also the sunlit meadows, shady wood paths, and the peace and great calm of a country place which has been loved and taken care of for three generations.*[27]

He clarified his vision further a few years later, "My idea of Winterthur is that it is a country estate Museum [that shows] the Americans of the future what a country place and farm were like."[28] Winterthur remains a great museum, garden, library, and graduate school. Fortunately these jewels are still displayed in their original crown, a setting of rare beauty and tranquility.

# 1. Early Settlement and Sophistication

**Opposite** | Sugar box (detail of fig. 6) | The intricately worked warrior on horseback depicted on the hasp (clasp) of the sugar box displays Edward Winslow's ability to work the metal with amazing skill and aesthetic prowess. Exacting details, including the sense of movement from the rider's sweeping costume and the horse's stride, mark it as a noteworthy example of superb chasing.

OVER TIME, CERTAIN PERSPECTIVES regarding the past can perpetuate false notions (or myths) that have become generally accepted as "truth." Until the last few decades of the twentieth century, such was the case with our understanding of the life and culture of America's early settlers, who, many erroneously believed, led colorless lives devoid of richness and finery. However, thanks to collectors (among them, Henry Francis du Pont), dealers, and scholars who were perceptive enough to recognize the aesthetic importance of objects exhibiting the artisanry of our early craftsmen, many of the myths surrounding early Americans, their life, and culture have subsequently been exploded. We now realize that the more prosperous colonists enjoyed, indeed demanded, a level of material comfort and aesthetic style imitative of their counterparts abroad, especially by the latter part of the seventeenth century. Valued possessions as well as important recorded documents have illuminated the daily lives of such men and women of means as Peter Woodbury (1640–1704) of Beverly, Massachusetts; Thomas Hart (d. 1731) of Lynnfield, Massachusetts; and John and Margaret Staniford (m. 1678) of Ipswich, Massachusetts. And, as new information comes to light, we continue to learn more about the original owners, the craftsmen who fashioned these artful yet useful objects, and their meaning within a contemporary social context.[1]

Although the yeomen and craftsmen who came to these shores brought few possessions, they did carry with them, in their minds and muscles, a wealth of knowledge and experience of the material and spiritual culture from whence they came. The aesthetic sen-

27

1 | *Differents Pourtraicts de Menuiserie* (Antwerp, 1588) | This illustration from a book by the noted late Renaissance designer Hans Vredeman de Vries documents the strong architectural style of furniture in the late sixteenth century that influenced objects made in seventeenth-century America.

2 | Hart Room | A room from the Thomas Hart house, built about 1670 in Ipswich, Massachusetts, and now installed at Winterthur, provides a fitting architectural context for Peter Woodbury's 1680 cupboard, an impressive turned armchair, and a cabinet made in 1676 for Thomas Buffington (1639 – 1728) and his wife Sarah Southwick (1644 – 1733) of Salem.

sibility they embraced had evolved from Renaissance principles of classical proportion and order, which by the sixteenth century had been transformed into an exaggerated style that is presently called mannerism (fig. 1). The overall forms and ornament of furniture and other useful objects often followed architectural precedents, sometimes resembling the highly ordered paneling seen in period interiors and sometimes echoing the outlines of entire building structures. With its geometrically organized central door with applied moldings, flanking arched panels, and bold overhanging upper section with pendant drops, the massive, highly ornamented cupboard shown in Winterthur's Hart Room (fig. 2) is a superb example of this style. This piece would have been a significant purchase even for a person of some means, and the relatively few surviving examples of cupboards of this stature (today often called court cupboards) testify to their importance in the period. Essentially the Cadillac (or Mercedes) of sideboards, this piece would have firmly proclaimed both status and wealth. Peter Woodbury, the original owner who was referred to as a yeoman (farmer/landowner) in his will and inventory, was a significant landowner who owned at least one enslaved African American (called Black Robin) and whose estate was valued at over £480, a significant amount in 1704.[2]

If a massive, elaborately fashioned and ornamented cupboard represented the height of vanity furniture in a late seventeenth-century household, a further pronouncement of status might well be evidenced by the possessions displayed on such a piece of fur-

niture. For example, when Giles Mode of Virginia died in 1657, his inventory listed "two glasses and whyte earthen ware on the cupboardshead."[3] Since only the simplest types of utilitarian ceramic vessels were actually made in seventeenth-century America, imported wares, especially drinking vessels, were commonplace in well-to-do households.

Archaeological evidence in the form of excavated shards (such as broken and discarded plates or pots) also tells us much about what was owned and used in homes from South Carolina and Virginia, to New Netherland and New England. Although such evidence usually points to German stonewares and to English and Dutch tin-glazed earthenwares, it also indicates, as do period documents, that some Chinese export hard-paste porcelains had made their way to America as early as the 1620s.[4] The written records, however, must be interpreted with care. For instance, the Cheney cup cited in Nicholas Toop's 1679 York County, Virginia, inventory might have been porcelain,[5] but it could also have been Dutch tin-glazed earthenware decorated in imitation of Chinese porcelain, as in the case of a punch bowl dated 1668 (fig. 3). However, the "China Disshes" (some "crakt & broke") recorded in quantity in the 1695 inventory of Rev. Rudolphus Van Varick and his wife Magrita, of Long Island, New York, were, judging from their high values, undoubtedly Chinese.[6] The popularity of imported Chinese porcelains with blue-and-white decoration prompted the competitive production in England and on the Continent of tin-glazed earthenwares with decorative motifs in imitation of the hard-paste wares.

A wide assortment of necessary objects fashioned out of brass and copper was also imported from England and the Continent. Colonial merchants in a well-documented trade sold imported chandeliers, candlesticks, snuffers with trays, elaborately engraved tobacco boxes, chafing dishes, pipe tongs, bed-warming pans, kettles, skillets, and numerous other esoteric, yet essential items. Early settlers arriving in America may also have brought a few precious brass objects, like candlesticks (fig. 4). Until the first quarter of the eighteenth century, very little brass or copper was produced locally, and even as founders and braziers established themselves, they often could not compete with better and less costly imported goods. By 1700 the amount of brass shipped to America from England alone totaled twenty-eight tons.[7] Seventeenth-century inventories also indicate that quantities of brass were imported. When "Peter Hobart late Minister of the Gosple in the Town . Of Hingham . In New-England" died in 1678, his inventory listed "two small brass candlesticks. 3/s. one tin.candlestick. Sawcer tin pan. And pottinger .2/s.2.d....three cast brass skillets & one small mortar and pestel." And when Capt. Samuel Ruggles, innkeeper of Roxbury, Massachusetts, died in 1692, he had "In Brass, Three Kettles, 5 Skillets, a warming pan...4 brass Candlesticks."[8] Although determining exactly where these objects were made and what they looked like is impossible, these references do document a wide range of forms and values, suggesting that some may have originally been of significant aesthetic merit.

Perhaps one of the rarest luxury items imported for use in seventeenth- and early eighteenth-century American households was the carpet. A member of the Cogswell family in Essex, Massachusetts, had by 1676, "a Turkey worked carpet in Old England, which he commonly used to lay upon his parlour table."[9] Not only is written documentation of such excess scarce, but pictorial images are even rarer.[10] All manner of imported, showy extravagances are brilliantly displayed in *Unknown Woman* (fig. 5) from New Amsterdam (New York City), whose riveting likeness was probably painted by Gerret Duyckinck (1660–1710). Although the identity of this comely young woman has never been firmly ascertained,[11] the creation of this image was indisputably purposeful and quite consciously directed to send a strong message. The carpet, her ivory framed fan, the rich lace and silk fabric of her gown, and her gold ring, necklace, and earrings

**4** | Candlesticks, Nuremberg, Germany, 1650–1690 | This pair of late seventeenth-century candlesticks represents the type of European metalwares that Americans used in their homes during the period of early settlement. Although a few founders and braziers established themselves in America, they often could not compete with better, less costly goods imported from Europe.

all suggest her wealth and position in society. What meaning then is presented by the young girl's prominent offering of the red carnation? In Renaissance portraiture, a red carnation held in the subject's hand commemorates betrothal; therefore, this image may well have been a wedding portrait.[12]

As is customary today, occasions such as marriages and births were often marked by the gift of very special, precious objects, including a rare late seventeenth- and early eighteenth-century form known as a sugar box. Of all the specialized forms fashioned by silversmiths, the sugar box must have been the most challenging. Only nine American examples survive today, and compelling evidence suggests that not many more were then made in this country. Certainly some settlers may have carried to these shores ones made abroad, such as the "great siluer trunke with 4 knop to st[a]nd on the table with suger" that Elizabeth Glover brought from London in 1638.[13] Winterthur's sugar box (fig. 6), one of the most splendidly ornamented examples, was presented to Daniel Oliver (1664–1732) and Elizabeth Belcher (1678–1735) in 1702 upon the birth of their son. Its maker, the Boston silversmith Edward Winslow, also fashioned three other sugar boxes, two of which were wedding presents. It is in the design and execution of these masterful treasures that the extraordinary capabilities of urban American artisans triumph. The complexly worked imagery on these boxes is symbolic of courtly love, chivalry, marriage, and fecundity, all appropriate representations on marriage and birth gifts (see detail of fig. 6). An interesting custom linked sugar boxes and marriage: drinking liquor and eating lumps of liquor-soaked sugar was a courtship ritual. Samuel Sewall, the noted New England diarist, recalled his courtship of Katherine Brattle Eyre Winthrop, recording that although his suit was unsuccessful, "She gave me a Dram of Black-Cherry Brandy, and gave me a lump of the Sugar that was in it."[14]

Seventeenth-century American drinking vessels, the spirituous liquors they held, and the customs that accompanied the imbibing of such liquors not surprisingly derived from English and Continental precedents. The sources for much of the form and ornament of these objects can be found in Italian Renaissance and mannerist engravings and objects. The sizes of these vessels varied, ranging from smaller ones conceived for individual use to larger ones shared among guests. Bulbous bodies, often ornamented with engraved or chased decoration, meant increased capacity. Curved cast handles with foliate or figural decoration (rather than smoothly finished surfaces) decreased the risk of a vessel's slipping from the greasy grip of a slightly tipsy merrymaker.

Robert Sanderson Sr. (1608–1693), who had been admitted to London's Worshipful Company of Goldsmiths in 1632, was the first trained silversmith to come to the

**5** | *Unknown Woman*, attributed to Gerret Duyckinck, New York, 1690–1700 | Gerret Duyckinck's painting of an unknown woman sheds light on the surroundings of the wealthy in New Amsterdam at the turn of the eighteenth century. Duyckinck, a noted citizen of New Amsterdam, was familiar with costly goods such as heavily patterned textiles, airy lace cuffs and collar, and gold and coral jewelry.

**6** | Sugar box, Edward Winslow, Boston, 1702 | William Partridge gave this sugar box to Daniel Oliver and Elizabeth Belcher in honor of the birth of their first son, Daniel, who died soon after. Inherited by a younger son, Peter, it was taken to England when he left Massachusetts as a British sympathizer, which fact suggests that it held not only great monetary value, but familial value as well.

colonies. Arriving in America in 1638, he apparently did not resume his craft until 1652, when in Boston, Massachusetts, he founded with partner John Hull America's first mint. His substantial caudle cup (fig. 7) with caryatid handles (stylized female figures) is testimony to his skill in smithing as well as in chasing. Though greatly worn by use over centuries, the chased ornament was drawn from late sixteenth- or early seventeenth-century illustrations of exotic flora and fauna. Curiously, the central ornament chosen for one side is a turkey, a wild fowl recognized as an exotic bird by naturalist and mannerist engravers.[15] Although this cup does not have a cover, the form was sometimes fashioned with a cover, such as the "1 Coadle cupp with cover" noted in the 1675 inventory of John Freake (1635–1675) of Boston.[16] A popular drink that could be made with a variety of ingredients, caudle was essentially a slightly thickened, sweetened, and spiced concoction that might contain ale, white wine, or brandy. This brew was often served warm, hence the need for a cover. In 1848 Boston's renowned statesman Oliver Wendell Holmes wrote a poem "On Lending a Punch Bowl" in *The Autocrat of the Breakfast Table,* noting that said bowl "T'was filled with caudle spiced and hot, and handed smoking round."[17]

The New York two-handled covered cup made by Jurian Blanck Jr. (fig. 8) is a tour de force of design and execution, with engraving, chasing, and repoussé ornament; this cup was undoubtedly a most costly object, emblematic not only of aesthetic value but also of wealth. It may have been a nuptial present to Jacobus and Eva (Philipse) Van Cortlandt, who married in 1691 and whose initials appear on the side and bottom of the cup.[18] The elaborately engraved coat of arms are those of the Philipse family, suggesting that the cup may have been commissioned by Eva's father, Frederick Philipse, who was possibly the richest man in New York when he died in 1702. Distinctly modeled after an English form, these cups may have been used for sipping syllabub, another sweet, spirituous concoction.

**9** | Two-handled bowl, Jacob Ten Eyck, New York, about 1735 | Although made more than fifty years later in a different colony, Jacob Ten Eyck's double-handled bowl is similar to Sanderson's caudle cup (fig. 7): both employ traditional European forms, which were rare and expensive in America. However, each vessel shows regional variation and individual artistic interpretation.

In direct contrast to the very Anglo-American interpretation of Blanck's covered cup is the Dutch-derived form of Jacob Ten Eyck's two-handled, paneled brandywine bowl *(brandewijnskom)* (fig. 9). A popular form in the Netherlands from the mid-seventeenth century into the nineteenth century, these bowls were customarily filled with brandy and raisins, and passed from guest to guest at festive celebrations usually marking a marriage or the safe delivery of a newborn. Caryatid handles similar to those derived from Renaissance precedents on the Sanderson caudle cup were referred to as "two cast Ears with Heads upon them" in a 1733 newspaper notice describing silver stolen in Flatbush, New York.[19]

Silver drinking vessels denoted a certain level of status, regardless of what drink they contained. Indeed in colonial society, beer was a beverage principally consumed by gentlemen, and wealthier sorts drank from silver tankards, mugs, cups, or beakers. More middling and lower sorts would have perhaps drunk cider from vessels of pewter, wood, leather, earthenware, or stoneware. Inventories of men of status frequently contained quantities of "plate," as wrought silver was called in the seventeenth and eighteenth century. Tankards always had hinged covers with convenient thumbpieces that enabled a user to hold it in one hand and easily raise the lid with a thumb while lifting the vessel to the lips. Covers assured that flies or other noisome bugs stayed out of the beverage when attention was directed toward other amusements or business. Mugs and beakers were also used for beer, ale, and cider, but these cups were typically without covers. Tankards in the late seventeenth and early eighteenth century were generally stout, flat-lidded forms. Boston silversmiths such as John Coney followed English designs with little ornament and occasionally engraved lids (fig. 10). New York silversmiths, however, emulated Dutch precedents for their patrons by ornamenting the bases of their tankards with elaborate applied foliate bands and embellishing the handles with cast ornament sometimes in the form of rampant lions. About 1710 Dutch-born

silversmith Jacob Boelen fashioned an impressive tankard (fig. 11) in this distinctly New York style for the marriage of Evert and Engletie Wendell of Albany.

The objects created by seventeenth-century artisans bespeak much about aesthetics, customs, lifestyles, available materials, and, occasionally, the original owners, particularly when items descended in early families are marked with initials. However, excepting silversmiths, who frequently stamped their pieces with their mark, the craftsmen who designed and executed most other objects have remained largely unidentified until recently. Although the names and work of a few early furniture joiners have long been known, defining groups and schools (based on a combination of historical records, regional provenances, and family ties) has been a challenge for recent generations of scholars. Frequently, the English or European background of a family of artisans is of key importance, providing crucial evidence of the design and craft traditions that they learned abroad and brought with them. Over the past three decades, several scholars have identified a seventeenth-century school of joiners in Salem, Massachusetts, focused around John Symonds (c. 1595–1671) and his sons James (1633–1714) and Samuel (1638–1722).[20] About 1636 the elder Symonds emigrated from Great Yarmouth, Norfolk, England; interestingly, the interior architectural paneling found there is strikingly similar to furniture attributed to the Symonds school in Salem. Although not the major urban center that Boston was, Salem, along with other nearby towns including Newbury and Ipswich, provided a ready bevy of craftsmen.

The production of these talented joiners ranged from seating furniture to cupboards, chests, and small cabinets. It is a tribute to Henry Francis du Pont's keen collecting eye that he acquired not just one, but two of the rarest of seventeenth-century forms, the diminutive valuables cabinet, or, as they were sometimes called in the period, case of drawers or chest of boxes (fig. 12). Made three years apart presumably in the Symonds shop in Salem, each cabinet is marked on the face of the door with the date (1676 and 1679) and the original owner's initials (for Thomas and Sarah Buffington, and Thomas Hart, respectively). Although at first glance these small locked cabinets seem quite different, they are actually remarkably similar and bear the classic architectural design and ornamental features associated with the Symonds shop: intricately carved sides, front door panels with applied moldings, split-turnings, corbels, and small turned ball feet. Inside each case are ten drawers of varying sizes, each appropriate for holding jewelry, money, documents, and other sundry valuables owned by both men and women. Four cabinets bearing the initials of their original owners and relevant dates are currently known, and all are attributed to the Symonds shop.[21]

**10, 11** | Tankard (right), John Coney, Boston, about 1690; Lid (detail of Coney tankard); Tankard (top left), Jacob Boelen, New York, about 1710 | The similarity between these stout and massive tankards ends with their flat lids and boldly curved handles. Each expresses a distinctive regional style through its engraved and applied ornament: The whimsical cherub emerging from a flower blossom and encircled by a foliate scroll is an ornamental device used not only by Coney (on several pieces) but also by other Boston silversmiths. And the cast, applied base molding on Boelen's tankard instantly identifies it as a New York product.

Perhaps equally as prized today as they were by their original seventeenth-century owners are joined armchairs, or joined great chairs, as they were usually called during the period. As is true for present-day households, various forms of seating furniture were present in seventeenth-century homes, though the most common types appear to have been side chairs and small stools. Another seating style used in conjunction with great long tables—though rarely known to survive today—was the "form" or long bench. Between 1635 and 1681, household inventories taken in Essex County, Massachusetts, alone enumerated only 22 great joined chairs, as compared to 1,598 chairs, 289 stools, 291 joined stools, 175 forms, and 11 benches.[22] In 1683 when Capt. Daniel Fisher of Dedham, Massachusetts, died, his inventory included "In the Parlour...the great table, Forme, and three joined stooles" valued at £02.05.3, "a small table & a joined chaire. 3.great turned chaires and five small chaires" at £01.14.9, and "a livery cupboard and what appertain's thereunto" at £02.10.00.[23] Not every household would have had a joined chair, as did Captain Fisher's, but some might have had more than one. Today these great joined armchairs appear to be quite hard and uncomfortable, but originally most would have been furnished with fabric-covered cushions filled with feathers.

**12** | Cabinets, attributed to the Symonds shop, Salem, Massachusetts, 1676 and 1679 | These diminutive storage cabinets, fitted with locks for securing valuables, represent a rare furniture form in seventeenth-century New England. Marked with the initials of their owners and dates of manufacture, they were doubtless specially commissioned objects.

Winterthur's joined great chair (fig. 13), made in Essex County, Massachusetts, is one of six known closely related examples—all are owned today by major institutions.[24] Similar form, construction, and materials potentially link these six great chairs to the same shop; all were made identically using what is referred to as a rail-and-stile construction held together with mortise and tenon joints secured by wooden pins. Hence the chairs echo the low, boxy, rectilinear form of rail-and-stile chests of the same period. Variations in the decorative carving across the upper portion of the back of the chairs, however, suggest that they were not all carved by the same hand. The motifs of lunettes, or arches, S-scrolls, and stylized foliage are all found variously on carved chests and boxes of the same period from Essex County.

Judging from surviving examples, turned armchairs, or great chairs, with flag or rush bottoms were apparently produced in greater variety and larger numbers than carved and joined armchairs, which required greater skill and more labor, and therefore cost more money. The talents of a different type of craftsman, the skilled turner, were required in the fashioning of turned chairs, which were less labor intensive and therefore less costly. Turned armchairs were probably found in homes where the resources were not available to own a joined armchair; more prosperous households might have had both. Winterthur's most impressive turned great chair (fig. 14) is a remarkably substantial chair with sixteen crisply turned spindles in the back and below the arms. Furniture of this early period was keenly collected by the late nineteenth and early

**13** | Armchair, Essex County, Massachusetts, 1640–1685 | This joined great chair, made using rail-and-stile construction secured with mortise and tenon joints, represents a costly investment for a seventeenth-century household. That so few survive today further supports their rarity and costliness.

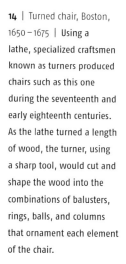

**14** | Turned chair, Boston, 1650–1675 | Using a lathe, specialized craftsmen known as turners produced chairs such as this one during the seventeenth and early eighteenth centuries. As the lathe turned a length of wood, the turner, using a sharp tool, would cut and shape the wood into the combinations of balusters, rings, balls, and columns that ornament each element of the chair.

twentieth centuries, consequently many significant examples were already out of circulation and in collections by the time H.F. du Pont began buying in the 1920s. He paid the record sum (at that time) of $4,000 for this armchair, which was acquired at the sale of the collection of Philip Flayderman in 1930. Although the wide variety of shapes and styles of turning makes specific regional and more precise shop attributions difficult, furniture scholars are progressively making inroads in these studies as provenances are examined and new information about relationships between makers and patrons is discovered.

The provenance of the earliest known dated American chest of drawers (fig. 15) is impeccable. Dated 1678 and bearing the carved initials "JSM," it was made for John and Margaret Staniford of Ipswich, Massachusetts, who married in 1678. The chest has traditionally been attributed to English joiner Thomas Dennis (1638–1706), who came from Devonshire, England, about 1663. This attribution was based on several facts ascertained by the late Benno M. Forman: Dennis was the only joiner known to be working in Ipswich at the date carved on the chest; John Staniford's wife's family were Dennis' next-door neighbors; and both John and Margaret Staniford witnessed Dennis' will in 1706.[25] Du Pont acquired this significant chest in 1930 directly from Alice Heard, a fifth-generation descendant of the original owners.[26]

Chests with lids and chests over drawers were the most common form of case furniture throughout the seventeenth century. Not until the last quarter of the century were cases fitted with tiers of long drawers made in America. The overall design and ornamentation of the Staniford piece are distinctive among early chests of drawers. Although over the centuries it has been subjected to some minor alterations and additions of decoration (for instance some of the polychrome decoration is now thought to be of later date), the overall original intent and integrity remain as an unparalleled example of late seventeenth-century casework. The construction using five tiers of drawers is unusual for case furniture of the last quarter of the seventeenth century. Additionally, the alternating bipartite and tripartite organization of the drawer façades is distinctive, as is the combination of turned applied parts and carved decoration.[27] Although originally the façade of this chest of drawers may have been more a harmony of ebonized turnings and monochromatic woods, the tradition of painted sixteenth- and seventeenth-century furniture was well-established in England, and therefore a limited repertoire of polychrome might be expected. Certainly the innovative, creative organization and ornament of this case of drawers mark it as a unique triumph, whether by Dennis or by an as yet unnamed craftsman.

More than a quarter century later and some 130 miles to the west in the upper Connecticut River valley, a Hadley, Massachusetts, chest of drawers (fig. 16) was made in the same tradition of joinery and ornamental creativity as the Staniford 1678 chest of drawers (fig. 15). Heavy corner posts framing side panels, framed rear panels, and side-hung drawers echo the seventeenth-century manner of construction of the earlier chest. Yet the ordered, repetitive symmetry of the compass-formulated spherical orbs decorating the drawer façades is conceptually different from the varied ornament and organization of the former piece. In essence the Hadley chest of drawers looks backward in its construction, yet forward in its ornament. As furniture historian Philip Zea has aptly stated, it "illustrates the marriage of the traditional technology of joinery with new design concepts."[28] He further compares the painted drawer fronts with their defined banded borders to the repetitive effect of baroque (William and Mary) veneered case furniture, in which flitches (sheets of veneer) repeat the design and the whole is enclosed by bands of herringbone veneer. This type of highly patterned, veneered furniture was made in urban areas, where such choice materials were readily available, at about the time the Hadley chest of drawers was fashioned. What did the nonurban artisan who created this piece see that inspired him? Was it the patron who dictated the concept based on a sojourn he had made to areas beyond the local realm of the craftsman? Several other surviving pieces with closely related decorative motifs hail from the same region, and possibly the same shop, including a monumental cupboard made

**15** | Chest of drawers, Essex County, Massachusetts, 1678 | The form of a chest, or case, of drawers was introduced into America in the last quarter of the seventeenth century. This example relates to a distinctive group of cupboards and chests of drawers recently suggested as the work of a northern Essex County shop.

**16** | Chest of drawers, Hadley, Massachusetts, 1710 – 1720 | The symmetrical pattern and originally vivid colors ornamenting this nonurban, western Massachusetts chest of drawers subtly suggest the bold, baroque decoration of more costly urban products.

for Hannah Barnard (about 1715) and a chest over drawers.[29] As in the Hadley chest of drawers, the joinery of these pieces clings to tradition, while the design concepts reach for contemporary inspiration.

Differing from the boxy, rectilinear, two-dimensional style of the seventeenth century, a new-fashioned style featuring lighter, more elongated elements and more sculptural turnings and carving prevailed in America in the first three decades of the eighteenth century. Although today art historians and decorative arts scholars use the term early baroque to characterize this style, it is most frequently referred to as William and Mary, after the monarchs who ascended to the throne of England in 1689. Introduced into England by Huguenot designers and craftsmen who flocked to the new court, the style soon spread to the colonies, where changes in forms and ornament were appearing by the 1690s. In major urban centers, the heavy mortise and tenon joinery, and stocky, bold turning of the seventeenth century were soon supplanted by a newer dovetailed board construction and more slender, articulated turning. New forms of case furniture were introduced, and high chests and dressing tables (see fig. 20) raised on delicately turned legs were produced, in addition to the new fashioned chests of drawers. Surface ornament changed as carving became more three-dimensional and the flat surfaces of case furniture were veneered with highly figured wood or painted in imitation of figured woods and Chinese lacquerwork. Such forms and ornament are found throughout Winterthur's Wentworth Room (fig. 17), in which Henry Francis du Pont aptly evoked the aura of this style.

A ready source of designs in the new style was provided by the English and Continental furniture imported to American coastal urban areas, where both patrons and artisans took note. An excellent example of this influence is seen in the impact that turned cane-back and cane-bottom chairs and couches imported from London had on colonial seating furniture.[30] Cane furniture was shipped in large quantities to New England and the middle colonies in the last two decades of the seventeenth century; it was probably imported into southern areas even earlier. The Boston armchair (fig. 18) is a fine example not only of the William and Mary style, but also of the influence of London-made, cane-back chairs. Though upholstered in leather, this chair has a carved crest and carved front stretcher similar in aspect to imported examples. Its high, attenuated back, more sculptural, carved crest and front stretcher, and the more slender, shapely turnings herald the new style. The turned members of this William and Mary armchair are vastly different in thickness, rigidity, and mass from those of the Essex County joined great chair (fig. 13). The later, leather upholstered armchair looks more comfortable with its rear stiles canted backward above the seat rails. The elegantly shaped arms with front

**18** | Armchair, Boston, 1695–1710 | Distinctly inspired by colonial imports of London carved-back, cane-seated furniture, this strongly vertical armchair reflects styles introduced by Huguenot designers who had immigrated to England following the ascension of William and Mary in 1689.

**19** | Armchair, Philadelphia, 1690–1720 | Although related in style to the Boston leather-upholstered, maple armchair (on the left), this Philadelphia-made chair reflects its region of manufacture in the use of native black walnut.

scrolled terminals also define the new style, which was moving away from the rigidity of seventeenth-century design toward a more curvilinear form. The importance of this superb armchair lies not only in its overall proportion, execution and design, but also in its upholstery, which is the original Russia leather used by its maker. Made from reindeer hides probably imported from Siberia, this leather was more supple and durable, presumably because of a special tanning process, and more costly because the hides were shipped via Europe from Saint Petersburg, Russia.[31]

Chairmakers in the middle colonies also rose to meet the competition from imported London cane-back seating furniture. An impressive example is seen in a Philadelphia armchair (fig. 19). With its high back, rear stiles canted above the seat rails, and curved arms with scrolled terminals, it relates in overall style to the leather-covered Boston armchair. Yet it has some very distinctive features: turned front posts with heavy inverted baluster shape and carved front feet, often referred to as Spanish feet, which are a characteristic of the William and Mary style. The history of ownership in the Lloyd family of Philadelphia and the liberal use of black walnut, a native wood commonly found in more costly Philadelphia furniture of this period, support an attribution to a Philadelphia maker. However, the small amount of cane-seated furniture identified as

Philadelphia-made (compared to the much greater number of New England examples) makes this armchair a very significant example of the William and Mary style in the middle colonies.

An exceptional example of the William and Mary style—especially its new form, overall lightness in mass, play of pattern on the flat surface of case furniture, and newer construction technique using dovetails instead of framed members joined with mortise and tenon construction—is seen in a dressing table from Boston (fig. 20). The rich surface treatment of this piece, whose façade and top are ornamented in a highly figured burl walnut veneer, is also seen in a related high chest in the Wentworth Room at Winterthur (fig. 17). On the dressing table, each drawer front is "framed" by a band of so-called herringbone veneer that contrasts with the more randomly figured burl. This contrast of patterns is repeated in the juxtaposition of the mass of the case versus the void of open space beneath. Likewise, the shape of the cuplike turnings on the top of the leg turnings is echoed in the arches across the lower edge of the case. The serpentine stretchers further repeat this shape and enhance the burgeoning curvilinear aspect of this style. Hence the overall curvilinear form in case furniture is emblematic of the early baroque or William and Mary style. Even the delicate brasses with baluster-shaped drops repeat the lightness and sculptural play of this period.

**20** | Dressing table, Boston, 1700–1725 | The dramatic use of walnut burl veneer on this dressing table is indicative of the shift to highly patterned surfaces on high style William and Mary case furniture. The turned legs also reflect a shift to lighter, more curvilinear designs.

21 | *Magdalena Douw (Mrs. Harme Gansevoort),* artist unknown, New York, about 1740 | This image of Magdalena Douw not only describes the material richness and social prowess of the sitter, but also successfully captures the visual boldness of baroque design, which enhanced everything from furniture to fabrics during the period.

The increasingly rich, sumptuous, and curvilinear nature of early eighteenth-century design is similarly displayed in the captivating portrait (fig. 21) of young Magdalena Douw (1718–1796), a fourth generation descendant of Dutch settlers.[32] Movement permeates this image, from the playful curves of her brilliant red shoes, upward through the trailing foliate designs of her obviously expensive gown (probably woven silk), to the ruffled lace trim and bonnet, and off the canvas with the arches of the background portals. Even the bulbous bold turnings of the three-legged stand are echoed in the spherical curves of the fruit in the basket and the cherries she holds in her hand. In 1740 Magdalena married Harme Gansevoort, a prosperous merchant with an equally distinguished Dutch lineage who also inherited his father's Albany brewery.

This portrait is thought to have been painted just prior to her marriage, and the cherries and fruit basket perhaps refer to abundance and fecundity for the impending union (in the decades that followed, Magdalena bore nine children, four of whom lived to maturity). Perhaps emanating from the Netherlandish tradition of genre and portrait painting, this charming glimpse into the traditions and richness of the Hudson Valley's Dutch mercantile society bespeaks of Douw's position. As a social document, it tells the viewer that Magdalena (and her new husband) recognized the status that portraiture held, and they chose to spend their resources on a form that had social, rather than monetary, value.

The emergence of the sumptuous early baroque style carried with it elements drawn from a sixteenth- and seventeenth-century vocabulary of design (fig. 22), some of which are readily seen in the great grisaille-painted *kasten* (see fig. 23) produced in the New World, presumably in New York City.[33] Echoing elements seen in Magdalena Douw's lively image, such as clusters of fruit, ribbon bowknots, and architectural arches, such painted storage cupboards were directly inspired by seventeenth-century Netherlandish interiors and furniture. Imitating more costly carved woodwork and furniture, the tradition of grisaille painting that flourished abroad was to a lesser extent embraced in colonial New York. Although today few Netherlandish examples survive that document this popular practice, it is known that a substantial production of softwood furniture was decorated in imitation of more costly carved hardwood pieces. In Amsterdam this painted, softwood furniture was made exclusively by *witwerkers*.

**22 | *Officina Archularia*,** Crispijn van de Passe (Amsterdam, 1642) | Seventeenth-century engraved designs incorporating fruit and flowers into garlands and pendant clusters, such as those by van de Passe, provided inspiration for the Dutch craftsmen who decorated massive *kasten* with trompe l'oeil grisaille ornament.

The bold, trompe l'oeil ornament of these *kasten,* painted in black and white on a blue-gray background, harks back to Italian Renaissance Della Robbia images of fruitful abundance. On this *kast* (fig. 23), the pomegranate centered in the pendant cluster of fruit framed within the niche is a symbol of fertility. Scholars of this furniture form have suggested that *kasten* were made for young women as dowry pieces.[34] Their function as major pieces for the storage of household textiles would support this supposition. The Dutch were noted for not only their cleanliness, but also their orderliness; their household guides suggested placing two strips of cloth on the shelves of cupboards, or *kasten*—one to keep the linen from touching the wood of the shelf and the other to cover it. The New York inventory of Jacob De Lange, for instance, lists "six cloths which they put upon the boards in the case."[35] Like New England cupboards of the seventeenth century that displayed costly and showy objects of status, *kasten* presumably also held imported, prized possessions. Evert Van Hook of New York willed to his wife in 1711 "the new cupboard that is now amaking by Mr. Shaveltie, and the three great and twelve small earthen cups, that stand on top of said cupboard." And Cornelius

**23** | *Kast,* New York, 1700 – 1735 | Grisaille-painted *kasten,* usually made of poplar, had a plain door that provided a flat surface for painting. Grisaille, a French term for gray tones, is a painting technique that imitates a sense of depth, light, and shadow. Here, a pomegranate serves as the focal point for the hanging fruit, although other fruits, such as pears, were used.

Van Duyn left his wife "the cupboard in the parlor, with the bowls thereon standing."[36]
The blue-and-white tin-glazed earthenware vases displayed atop Winterthur's grisaille-
painted *kast* (fig. 23) illustrate this practice and suggest the presence of these costly,
highly ornamental ensembles in New York households.

Although the wealth amassed by seventeenth- and early eighteenth-century colonial
merchants and entrepreneurs was often manifested in showy material possessions such
as textiles and imported brass and ceramics, the acquisition of plate (or wrought silver) was another way of both displaying wealth and putting it into convertible assets.
Frequently "estate planning," in the form of a will, included gifts and bequests of
domestic silver (either wealth or assets) to a church. Today surviving colonial churches
and synagogues hold some of the greatest collections of early silver, both domestic

and ecclesiastical. In 1711, the Second Church in Boston received three significant gifts from parishioners. Made especially for use by the church in the service of Holy Communion were a covered flagon (for wine) standing almost a foot tall and a pair of monumental Communion dishes measuring over fifteen inches in diameter (fig. 24).[37] The flagon was the bequest of Elizabeth Paddy Wensley, who died in February 1710/1711.[38] Her husband was John Wensley, a mariner whose inventory at his death in 1686 totaled £1,762, a considerable sum. He left a house in the north end of Boston, wharves, and warehouses, which were all divided equally between his wife, son, and three daughters. Wensley's wealth is further confirmed by some of the possessions listed among his household goods, including eighteen Turkey work chairs in the hall and twenty-five leather chairs in the middle room.[39] It is not surprising that the maker of the flagon was Elizabeth Wensley's son-in-law, the silversmith Peter Oliver. An elegantly engraved inscription in a symmetrical foliate surround on the front of the flagon identifies this piece as Elizabeth Wensley's gift (see detail of fig. 24). The wealth and status of the Wensleys is further confirmed by the likenesses that were painted of them perhaps soon after their marriage in the early 1660s. Mrs. Wensley's elegant dress, along with the fan she holds in one hand, and the flowers, vine, and tree in the landscape background symbolize her gender, position, and marital status. A companion portrait of her husband, richly dressed with books in hand and on a table beside him, also announces his status, in particular, his wealth and education.[40]

The two Communion plates were made by silversmith Edward Winslow and were not a bequest to the Second Church, but the outright gift of two half brothers, Edward and Thomas Hutchinson. According to the inscription on the plates, this gift was made in May 1711 and may have been in some way related to the death of their father-in-law, John Foster, who had just died in February and who had lived on property adjoining that of Elizabeth Wensley. Neighbors and fellow parishioners of the Second Church, the Fosters, Wensleys, and Hutchinsons represented the second and third generation of colonial Americans who had prospered in the New World and not only enjoyed wealth in the material aspects of their daily lives, but also left legacies to the institutions that were the strongholds of their faith and society. Today, these emblems of wealth and benevolence survive in some of the same institutions, or in museums such as Winterthur, where they continue to represent the sumptuousness and sophistication of America's early settlers.

**24** | Chargers, Edward Winslow, Boston, 1711; Flagon, Peter Oliver, Boston, 1711; Inscription (detail of flagon) | The presentation of silver, whether given or bequeathed, was a way of donating assets to a church or synagogue. Sometimes domestic silver was bequeathed, but often pieces were commissioned specifically for ecclesiastical use, as was the case with these chargers (Communion plates) and flagon. Such gifts were often floridly engraved to document for posterity a donor's generosity.

# 2. East Meets West

**Opposite** | High chest (detail of fig. 1), John Pimm, Boston, 1740–1750 | The exoticism of the East is evoked in this great Boston pedimented high chest with japanned decoration. While the form is in the Queen Anne or late baroque style, the surface ornament exhibits a taste for the chinoiserie.

FOR CENTURIES, THE EXOTICISM OF THE EAST has fascinated Westerners. And its luxuries—tea, silk, spices, lacquerwares, and shimmering porcelains—have long been coveted by those wealthy enough to afford them. American colonists were no different from their counterparts abroad, and even in the seventeenth century, limited quantities of these goods made it to America's shores via Europe and England. Entrepreneurial merchants established companies, like the Dutch East India Company, specifically to trade with Far Eastern ports. And enterprising artisans both abroad and in the colonies created goods in imitation of Eastern wares in order to compete with the imports, to meet the demand for these costly commodities, and to capitalize on the profits from this lucrative trade. Later collectors have been as intrigued with these Eastern goods as their predecessors, and Henry Francis du Pont was no exception, for he was quite taken with a wide variety of objects made in or inspired by the East.

Some of the showiest and most costly wares imported to England and Europe from the East over the centuries were the lacquered, or japanned, pieces ranging from small boxes, brushes, and combs, to large-scale pieces of furniture. To capitalize on the craze for these wares, European and English craftsmen began to produce their own versions. A variety of publications in the period provided instructions to artisans and patterns for ornamentation. One of the more notable books was published in 1688 by two enterprising English artisans, John Stalker of London and George Parker of Oxford. Their work, *A Treatise of Japaning and Varnishing*, was essentially a how-to book describing in

**1** | Readbourne Parlor | Winterthur's impressive high chest made by Boston cabinetmaker John Pimm about 1750 is presented in the Readbourne Parlor, whose woodwork comes from a house of the same name built about 1733 on Maryland's eastern shore. Philadelphia furniture in the Queen Anne style complements the brilliantly japanned high chest, and a portrait of Experience Johnson Gouvernour (about 1750) by John Wollaston hangs over the fireplace.

great detail the tools, supplies, and techniques for "Guilding, Burnishing, Lackering" as well as the "best way of making all sorts of Varnish" and "Rules for Counterfeiting Tortoise-Shell, Marble, Staining & Dying Wood, Ivory, Horn." Following the eighty-four pages of instructive text in this volume (measuring 14⅜ × 9¼ in.) are "Above a hundred distinct Patterns for Japan-work—in imitation of the Indians for Tables, Stands, Frames, Cabinets, Boxes, &.... Curiously Engraven on 24 large Copper-Plates." Stalker and Parker even told readers not only how to trace these designs without harming the pages of the book, but also where to use them: "of Drawers som are Deepe & som more narrow of ye same cabbinett" (fig. 2). During the ensuing decades, a few other author-artisans followed suit with similar instructive manuals.

Artisans in the colonies also produced a type of highly ornamental lacquerwork similar to that described by Stalker and Parker. In Boston, the principal center for these wares, wealthy patrons commissioned some very impressive high chests (see fig. 1), dressing tables, bureau tables, tall clocks, and looking glasses beginning in the first decade of the eighteenth century. Although seating furniture was generally not japanned in the first half of the eighteenth century, a revival of this surface ornament occurred in the early nineteenth century, and at least two groups of side chairs were painted in imitation of japanned work (see fig. 4). Artisans in New York City japanned the cases of some tall clocks, and a small group of case furniture from the East Windsor region of Connecticut, north of Hartford, was decorated with a regionally distinctive interpretation of this decorative technique.[1]

Before 1750 at least ten artisans, called japanners, were working in Boston decorating case furniture with this elaborate surface ornamentation; three were working before 1730.[2] Although some high chests and at least one dressing table in the early eighteenth-century William and Mary style survive today, most of the known Boston japanned pieces are in the Queen Anne style, as it was during the height of that style's popularity that the taste for japanned work reached its zenith. The grandest and most impressive examples are a group of three high chests (one with a matching dressing table) with broken-scrolled pediments and carved and gilt shells in both the upper and lower cases.[3] Typical of the technique used in Boston japanning in the second quarter of the eighteenth century is a background painted brilliant vermilion, then overpainted with black in a mottled manner simulating tortoiseshell. In 1734 the Boston japanner William Randle charged cabinetmaker Nathaniel Holmes (1703–1774) for "Japanning a Piddement Chest & Table Tortoiseshell & Gold." Not only is this a very early reference to a pedimented high chest, but it is the earliest known reference to this type of tortoiseshell japanning in Boston.[4] Although the japanner who painted Winterthur's great

**2** | *A Treatise of Japaning and Varnishing,* John Stalker and George Parker (Oxford, England, 1688) | This treatise provided artisans with numerous designs for japanned ornament. Like the drawer decorations illustrated here, these drawings consist of numerous floral, animal, architectural, and natural motifs as well as images depicting scenes of Chinese men and women.

pedimented high chest (see fig. 1) is not known, the cabinetmaker who constructed the case was John Pimm (d. 1773). His identity is known today because he placed his name in chalk on the back of almost every drawer, presumably so that the japanner to whose shop he sent the piece for decoration would know to return it to "Pim."[5]

Representative of Boston japanning, the decorative motifs on this high chest range from Oriental figures in outdoor landscapes with fences and pavilions, to exotic birds, fantastic animals, and varied floral sprays. Some of these motifs are "raised," actually built up above the surface of the wood with gesso, then coated with gold to complete the overall effect of shimmery splendor. The great carved shells are gilt, as are the unusual (and costly) carved floral garlands beneath the shells. At the very top of the pediment, the decoration imitates the type of diaperwork often seen on Oriental lacquerwork. The square claw feet, a particularly unusual feature on this high chest, are somewhat related to the so-called Spanish feet seen on case furniture in the first half of the eighteenth century. We believe the original owner of this high chest was "Commodore" Joshua Loring (1716–1781), who in the 1740s became a privateer during the conflicts between England and France. It seems reasonable to imagine that Loring's purchase of this lavish, showy piece of furniture may have been made possible by the capture of a particularly profitable ship.

One of the most well-known Boston japanners was the multitalented artisan Thomas Johnston (1708–1767). In 1732 he engraved his own tradecard, a testimony to his talents, in which he called himself "Japaner…At the Golden Lyon," where he sold "Japan Work of all Sorts, As Chests of Drawers, Chamber & Dressing Tables, Tea Tables, Writeing Desks, Bookcases, Clock-Cases."[6] Johnston, and artisans like him, may have owned a copy of Stalker and Parker's treatise (though its presence in the colonies during the seventeenth or eighteenth century has not yet been documented) or another similar publication on japanning. Alternatively, he, as well as his patrons, may have been familiar with locally owned imported pieces either made in the Orient or fashioned on the Continent or in England. For example, an impressive japanned English desk and bookcase was owned in the Bowdoin family of Boston and passed into the Pitts and Warner families after the Revolution.[7]

Although Johnston's 1767 estate inventory noted "a pell [pile] of books [£] 14:19/." and a "Book of Herraldry 48/," without a specific listing we can only speculate about the nature and content of these volumes.[8] Furthermore, only one example of japanned work, a tall clock case, is labeled by Johnston, and that case has been completely overpainted.[9] Circumstantial evidence suggests that two other clock cases, one at Winterthur (fig. 3) and the other in the Henry Ford Museum, Dearborn, Michigan, may be his work.[10] Further supporting these attributions is a listing in his inventory of "3 Clock Cases 120/" amidst what were clearly his tools and stock in trade. The decoration on the japanned case housing the works of the Winterthur clock is an exceedingly superb example of both design and execution. This attribution to Johnston is strengthened by his relationship with the maker of the works, Gawen Brown, who came from London in 1748 and boarded with Johnston and his family until 1752. In 1749 Brown advertised that he kept his shop at Johnston's and had for sale clocks with japanned cases; these, presumably, were decorated by Johnston.[11]

3 | Tall clock, works by Gawen Brown, Boston, 1749–1755 | The japanned decoration on the door of this tall clock case is particularly detailed and finely executed, consisting of a series of separate vignettes that suggest dimensionality. The tortoiseshell effect, produced by mottling black paint over a reddish brown ground, is especially visible on the door and upper part of the hood.

4 | Side chair, Boston, 1735–1750 | The renewed popularity of japanned decoration during the nineteenth century is manifested by the later decoration on this eighteenth-century Queen Anne side chair. Samuel Pickering Gardner presumably enhanced these old-fashioned chairs with his family crest and japanned decoration at about the time of his marriage.

In the early nineteenth century, japanned decoration was also added to older furniture by owners who wished to update its design. For instance, Winterthur's Queen Anne walnut side chair (fig. 4), which is typical of many made in Boston from the 1730s to just before the Revolution, was not originally intended to be painted. This chair, along with others from the same set and another almost identical set, had descended to Samuel Pickering Gardner (1767–1843) of Salem by the early nineteenth century. It is believed that probably shortly after Gardner married Rebecca Russell Lowell, these two groups of side chairs received their japanned decoration.[12] In the center of the front seat rail, a chevron bisects the shield; this device is Gardner's family coat of arms, presumably copied by the japanner from his engraved bookplate. Interestingly, one group of these chairs is ornamented with a foliate scroll motif on the face of the rear stiles and down the legs, and the other group has grapes and grape leaves trailing down the stiles and legs. Presumably the latter decoration was inspired by similar grapevine motifs on imported Chinese lacquerwork produced from the 1780s until well into the nineteenth century.[13]

Among the most popular and influential exports from the East were hand-painted and printed cottons produced in India. For centuries the Indians had been making large quantities of these textiles for markets in Asia and the Middle East. By the mid-seventeenth century, as European trading companies were established, these goods had begun to flow into Europe, England, and eventually the colonies. Because all Indian cottons posed great competition for manufacturers in England and France, they were banned in those countries for much of the eighteenth century. Hence, the colonies provided an attractive and important market for these goods, which were often simply referred to as India chintz. By 1770 nearly 3,000 pieces of India chintz had been exported to New York for a total value of £3,731.4.0.[14] Most of this fabric would have been in the form of yardage for dress goods, though some may have been printed with borders for bed and window hangings.

The choicest and most expensive Indian cottons were hand-painted cloths produced on the southeastern Coromandel Coast of India and referred to as palampores.[15] This unusual name is believed to have derived from a Persian and Hindi word *palangposh*, which was "a kind of chintz bed-cover."[16] Although period documents often simply refer to these cotton bed furnishings as "India furniture chintz," or "superfine India Chintz Counterpaines," in 1702 the inventory of Mary Ritchards mentioned "1 Pallampore and 4 small Boxes—15/8."[17] A remarkably early palampore (fig. 5), made between 1690 and 1720, is possibly similar to the one owned by Mary Ritchards. London export records for 1700 document the shipment to Virginia of 100 palampores valued at £40.16.[18]

The extremely delicate, flowing floral and foliate patterns on these bed coverings were literally hand-painted onto the cotton: the mordants (natural substances used to make dyes fast to light and water) were applied with a split bamboo tool, and the resist (which prevented the dyes from coloring the cloth) was applied with an iron pen. Hence these cottons were also called *kalamkari*, which translated as penwork. One of the most popular designs is known today as a tree-of-life pattern because it usually features one large central trunk branching out to reveal a panoply of brilliant buds, blossoms, and foliage. Young Mary King of Philadelphia was undoubtedly inspired by one of these impressive palampores when she conceived her silk needlework picture (fig. 6) in 1754. The central tree, scrolling branches, large lobed blossoms, and feathery foliage all echo

**5** | Palampore, India, 1690–1720 | Textiles imported from the East, like this painted Indian cotton called a palampore, had a major impact on the designs fashionable in Europe and the American colonies during the eighteenth century. The tree of life seen on this bed covering remained popular throughout the eighteenth century.

**6** | Needlework picture, Mary King, Philadelphia, 1754 | In her lavishly detailed needlework picture, Mary King used silk and metallic threads in a variety of stitches to create a distinctive look. Although her work contains European-inspired designs, the overall feel of the piece indicates King was influenced by Indian printed cottons featuring the tree-of-life motif.

designs seen in Indian textiles, especially palampores of the eighteenth century. The foreground with strawberries and rabbits, and the lion and leopard are, however, more reminiscent of English needlework sources. The brilliant yellow silk background of Mary King's needlework recalls the strong yellow backgrounds of Indian painted cottons produced predominantly for Eastern markets.

7 | Quilt, eastern United States, 1795–1825 | This American interpretation of a tree-of-life palampore actually comprises myriad small pieces of printed fabric appliquéd onto a plain cotton ground and then quilted.

America began direct trade with India not long after the American Revolution concluded with the 1783 signing of the Treaty of Paris. The ship *United States* left Philadelphia in March 1784 to head for China, but her captain decided to land at Pondicherry on the Coromandel Coast of India. When this vessel, along with the ship *Pallas*, returned to Philadelphia in the fall of 1785, an advertisement appeared in the *Pennsylvania Gazette* offering "for Sale at the Stores of Willing, Morris and Swanwick... Patampores, or Bed Covers, Masulepalnam Handkerchiefs and Checks."[19] Such an imported Indian palampore undoubtedly provided the inspiration for the creation of a magnificent appliquéd quilt (fig. 7). Though certainly not as delicate and subtle in its execution as the Indian penwork palampores, this piecework quilt has a boldness and character that is even more distinctive because of the fabrics its creator used.

There is no doubt that this quilt was made in America, for several of the printed fabrics used in it can be identified as having been printed in Philadelphia at the calico printing manufactory of the English-trained printer John Hewson. A number of English printers had settled in the Philadelphia area before the Revolution, and by 1810 the *Niles Weekly Register* noted eight Pennsylvania cotton printing manufactories. Hewson, who arrived in Philadelphia in 1773, became one of the area's most successful entrepreneurs, and in the 1788 Grand Federal Procession, he and his family were featured on the twenty-ninth float sponsored by the Pennsylvania Society for the Encouragement of Manufacturers and the Useful Arts. A detailed description of that particular exhibit noted, "Behind the looms was fixed the apparatus of Mr. Hewson, printing muslins of an elegant chintz pattern, and Mr. Lang, designing and cutting prints for shauls; on the right was seated Mrs. Hewson and her 4 daughters, pencilling a piece of very neat sprigged chintz of Mr. Hewson's printing, all dressed in cottons of their own manufacture."[20] Although the woman who actually created this quilt (fig. 7) is not known, her desire to sew her own special version of an Indian palampore is undeniable, and her choice of the Hewson fabrics has left not only an important document, but also a beautiful, aesthetically significant object. That Hewson himself owned an India chintz bed quilt, which he bequeathed to his daughter Anne Hodgson, documents his inspiration for calicos resembling Indian cottons, which work so well in this self-styled tree-of-life quilt.[21]

During the second half of the eighteenth century, English textile manufacturers attempted to appeal to every taste, and exotic Chinese designs figured prominently in their repertoire of copperplate-printed fabrics appropriate for use as loose cases covering furniture and as window and bed hangings. Surviving examples used in American households testify that these textiles were very popular in the colonies and early republic. Although somewhat reminiscent of Indian chintzes with serpentine tree trunks and large, exotic blossoms, birds, and fruits, these English fabrics were distinctive. While many of the motifs were probably derived from designs published in the 1750s in a number of books—including Edwards and Darly's *New Book of Chinese Designs Calculated to Improve the Present Taste* (London, 1754), Paul Decker's *Chinese Architecture, Civil and Ornamental* (London, 1759), and William Chambers' *Designs of Chinese Buildings, Furniture, Dresses, Machines, and Utensils* (London, 1757)—some motifs were peppered with fantasy. Many of these textiles embody the sentiments expressed by the English publisher Robert Sayer, who wrote in *Ladies Amusement* (London, 1762) that "With Indian and Chinese subjects greater liberties may be taken, because Luxuriance of Fancy recommends their Productions more than Propriety, for in them is often seen a Butterfly supporting an Elephant, or Things equally absurd; yet from their gay Colouring and airy Disposition seldom fail to please."[22] Fishing, hunting, and being out of doors, perhaps in an exotic and luxuriant garden, are omnipresent in much of the imagery of these chinoiserie textiles. In the three principal scenes in one such fabric (fig. 8), a man hunts with his absurd beast (part man, part animal) beside him and his servant behind, carrying a quiver of arrows and the downed ducks; a woman seated in a garden with a pagoda in the background holds an exotic bird; and a gentleman fishes while his servant cleans the catch. All of these scenes depict leisure activities that the well-to-do could enjoy in their own free time.

The imagery of gardens, leisure, and fanciful activities also appears in another fabric (fig. 9), though its overall composition is quite different from the previous textile panel (fig. 8). Both designs depict men or women fishing, exotic flora and fauna, and pagoda-like garden pavilions or bridges. These charming scenes draw viewers into a world of beauty and relaxation, and with their "gay Colouring" and "airy Disposition" they "seldom fail to please." Hence, they would have been quite appropriate in a chamber for bed hangings, perhaps even on a bed whose canopy resembled a pagoda, such as the one illustrated on the 1771 tradecard of New York upholsterer Richard Kip Jr.[23] Kip presumably cribbed the design for the pagoda canopy with a reclining Chinaman perched under a pagoda-like roof from Thomas Chippendale's 1762 edition of *The Gentleman and Cabinet-Maker's Director* (pl. 33). Such exotic chinoiserie bedchambers were very much in vogue in the houses of the English nobility by the mid-eighteenth century;[24] however, no American bedsteads of this elaborate a design survive from this period.

Perhaps the most ubiquitous image of the Orient was that of the pagoda—a temple or pavilion used for public worship, most usually constructed in a towering, tapered, multitiered form with concave rooflines and bells dangling off the tips of each level. This form of architecture was virtually unheard of in Europe and the colonies, and the captains, supercargoes (purchasing agents), and crews of the ships that sailed to the Orient were captivated by these amazing structures. Even as early as the seventeenth century, Westerners could have known of pagodas through published images (fig. 10), like those in John Nieuhoff's *An Embassy from the East-India Company of the United Provinces, to the Grand Tartar Cham Emperour of China* (London, 1669). Perhaps the most memorable pagoda seen by Westerners who went to China was the famed nine-stage example on Whampoa Island at the mouth of the Pearl River. Replicas of pagodas were produced by the Chinese in a variety of materials—including jade, soapstone, ivory, and porcelain—and sold to Western visitors as expensive souvenirs of their travels.

**8, 9** | Plate-printed cottons (details), England, 1765–1775 and about 1785 | Portraying exotic flora and fauna and fanciful Chinese designs, English copperplate-printed cottons such as these evoked the popular chinoiserie taste of the second half of the eighteenth century. Often these textiles were used as bed hangings and furniture coverings; their bold fantastic patterns were appropriate accompaniments to the modern, rococo furniture.

**10** | *An Embassy from the East-India Company of the United Provinces, to the Grand Tartar Cham Emperour of China*, John Nieuhoff (London, 1669) | Books about China provided Europeans with a glimpse of the Asian countryside and knowledge of the lifestyle and culture of the Chinese. Pagodas, temples for public worship, captivated the Western imagination and were reproduced in a variety of media, including print, porcelain, and ivory.

**11** | Pagoda, China, 1785–1830 | This imposing porcelain pagoda, one of a pair, boasts intricate detail work in its blue underglaze decoration. A finely articulated painted fretwork door adorns each stage, or tier, and the fanciful decoration alternates between dragons and flowers. Even the railings are ornamented: small gilt wood finials top each porcelain fence post.

One of the earliest models of a Chinese pagoda in this country was brought by Samuel Shaw (1754–1794) on the vessel *Massachusetts* in 1793.[25] Standing nearly four feet high, carved of ivory, and ornamented with small metal or gilt wood bells hanging from all nine rooflines, this model is said to be a copy of the fifteenth-century porcelain pagoda built by Emperor Chen Tsu (Ming dynasty, 1368–1644) as a tribute to his mother.[26] The Shaw pagoda, now in the Metropolitan Museum of Art, is displayed in a case that may well have been designed by the noted Boston architect Charles Bulfinch (1763–1844) probably soon after its arrival in America.[27]

Shaw had also been the supercargo on the *Empress of China;* leaving New York in February 1784 and returning in May 1785, it was the first American ship to sail directly to China. He had kept a detailed journal describing this first voyage to the East, noting, "there are large pagodas or temples, where are a number of 'bonzes,' or priests, who perform daily worship. In these temples are various idols, in the form of men and women, but many times larger than life, and of more terrific appearance."[28] Another pagoda, one carved of soapstone and white jade, was brought back from China in 1801 and presented that year to the East India Marine Society (the forerunner of the Peabody Essex Museum) in Salem, Massachusetts, by Nathaniel Ingersoll.[29] The pair of Chinese porcelain pagodas at Winterthur (fig. 11), though lacking the venerable provenance of those imported by Shaw or Ingersoll, are distinguished from the others by size (they are the largest at five feet tall) and by material (they are made of hard-paste porcelain). As wealthy Americans began creating luxuriant and fanciful gardens by the early years of

68

the nineteenth century, they imported exotic plants from the Orient and even occasionally built pagoda-like pavilions or summer houses as temples of leisure. Another successful China trade merchant from Boston, Thomas Handasyd Perkins (1764–1844), was so taken with the idea of a pagoda that he constructed his poultry house in the shape of one.[30]

The consumer fascination with and demand for all manner of shapes, forms, and ornament reminiscent of the Orient was seemingly boundless. As English architect and designer William Chambers stated in his 1757 *Designs of Chinese Buildings*, "The boundless panegyricks which have been lavished upon the Chinese learning, policy, and arts shew with what power novelty attracts regard, and how naturally esteem swells into admiration."[31] This "Chinese taste," as it was called by designers and artisans in the period, might be applied to or embodied by almost any type of object. That this Chinese taste sometimes encompassed the whole scheme of decoration in a room is well known through written documentation and the intact survival of entire rooms in English country houses, yet this decorating phenomena is much more difficult to document in the colonies. However, the fact that a variety of useful and decorative objects were produced abroad for use there poses the possibility that some of these objects might also have been imported to the colonies, even if they were not used in the same en suite manner as they might have been in England or Europe. For example, Winterthur's elegantly proportioned andirons (fig. 12), with matching shovel and tongs, were most likely made in England, but could well have been exported to America. There, frequent advertisements by merchants referred to various brass items "just imported…late arrivals from Europe" or "from London and Bristol,…andirons, neat brass and iron head shovel and tongs."[32] Though the Winterthur andirons' cabriole legs with claw-and-ball feet and fluted-pillar form at first echo the rococo taste, the pagoda-like finials that top the pillars are actually very unusual and rarely seen.

**12** | Andirons, probably England, possibly Philadelphia, 1760–1780 | Although utilitarian in their purpose, these andirons indicate how Chinese-inspired decoration and style permeated all types of objects. Made in England, the andirons are surmounted by a twisted decorative element that was certainly inspired by the distinctive roofline of Chinese pagodas.

Brass founders' catalogues of the second half of the eighteenth century offer other insights into the myriad possibilities for exhibiting Chinese taste in interiors. Pagodas and latticework patterns can be found on everything, from monumental andirons to the seemingly most minute furniture hardware. Many examples of Chinese-inspired hardware made their way to craftsmen in the colonies and were used on their most costly and impressive case furniture. Some hardware was simply pierced with latticework, such as the brasses on the Providence chest-on-chest (see chapter 3, fig. 28), while others were as ornate as those on a Philadelphia high chest (see chapter 3, fig. 18) and on an example from a Birmingham brass founder's catalogue (fig. 13) of the 1770s.

**13** | Illustration, from *Catalogue of Escutcheons, Hinges, Drawer Pulls, Tea-chest Handles, Candlesticks, Etcetera* (probably Birmingham, England, about 1770) | The rococo and chinoiserie style brass furniture drawer pull, with pagoda top and pierced latticework beneath, was understandably the most costly item on this particular page of this Birmingham catalogue. Identical chinoiserie brasses ornament the Philadelphia high chest (see chapter 3, fig. 18) owned by the Gratzes.

Some twentieth-century collectors, including Henry Francis du Pont, were so enamoured with the Chinese taste that they created interiors (fig. 14) that completely embodied this expression, from the wallcoverings to the furniture. Although no colonial interiors can be cited that achieved quite this holistic an approach, some wealthy pre-Revolutionary colonial merchants fancied the Chinese taste and imported wallpapers in the Chinese fashion. In 1737 Boston merchant Thomas Hancock ordered a "Chinese paper" to be made in London for the great mansion that he had just built on Beacon Street overlooking the Boston Common. Hancock sent a sample of a paper from "a Room Lately Come over here," but noted that he desired his paper to be "well Done and as Cheap as Possible, and if they can make it more beautiful by adding more Birds flying here and there, with Some Landskips at the Bottom, Should like it well."[33] In 1761 Samuel Dexter built a house in Dedham, Massachusetts, and installed an actual Chinese manufactured paper that was very likely imported via London.[34]

The first Chinese wallpapers to be imported directly to America from the Orient were two sets that came onboard the *Empress of China* in 1785; the ship's captain, John Green, purchased them from the Chinese paper dealer, Eshing, for Philadelphian Robert Morris (1734–1806).[35] Apparently this paper was never sold by Morris, even though in 1787 George Washington broached the question of Morris' obtaining some Chinese paper for him when he wrote "It is possible I may avail myself of your kind offer of sending for India Paper for my new Room [the dining room at Mount Vernon], but assuming there is no opportunity to do it soon, I shall not, at this time, give the dimensions of it."[36] The story of the discovery of this paper is quite fascinating, for it was found in the early 1920s by Henry Davis Sleeper in the attic of the Elbridge Gerry House in Marblehead, Massachusetts, apparently still in the boxes in which it was shipped (with Morris' name on them). In 1923, as Sleeper expanded and enhanced the decoration of Beauport, his home in Gloucester, Massachusetts, he remodeled his Elizabethan hall to become a China trade room, using about half of this Chinese paper.[37] This installation occurred just about the time that Sleeper began working with du Pont on the interiors of Chestertown House; therefore Henry Francis quite possibly heard of Sleeper's great coup.[38]

Du Pont was strongly influenced by the impressive wallpaper in Sleeper's China trade room. When he added a major wing to Winterthur from 1928 to 1931, he was so taken with the idea of a room with Chinese wallpaper that he desired a similar setting in his own home. In August 1930, Henry and Ruth Wales du Pont visited Beauport, and Ruth wrote to her mother:

*Had a wonderful experience yesterday. We went to Gloucester & lunched with Harry Sleeper at his house. It is a thrilling experience and I longed for you....The most interesting room, or one of them, is a Chinese Room, entirely furnished in objects brought from the Orient by sea captains... wallpaper made for the American market by the Chinese.*[39]

**14** | (Overleaf) Chinese Parlor | This large and sumptuous room epitomizes H. F. du Pont's talent for interior decoration. The hand-painted Chinese wallpaper provides an effective backdrop for ceramics, silver, and furniture inspired by Chinese designs. Imported Chinese lacquerwork folding screens further enrich this ensemble of complementary objects.

**15** | China table, attributed to John Townsend, Newport, Rhode Island, 1785–1800; Looking glass, England, 1760–1780; Tea wares, China, about 1786–1795 | Made expressly to contain tea wares on its top, this tea (or china) table reflects Chinese design in its pierced gallery, stretcher, and brackets. The Chinese porcelain tea wares, decorated with ships prominently flying the American flag, were made for the American market. The ornate English looking glass, with a central pagoda motif flanked by exotic birds, also reflects Chinese designs.

Although du Pont was taken with the idea of using Chinese wallpaper, he was not so enamoured with everything that Sleeper had done in the actual appointments—like the tented, faux pagoda-like ceiling—of the room. Following Sleeper's death, Beauport was sold in the mid-1930s to Helena McCann, who sought du Pont's advice and approval when she wished to alter the China trade room. Du Pont's reply to McCann was that she should definitely proceed with her own remake of the room, as he thought Sleeper's version "distinctly bad."[40]

Du Pont used a Chinese wallpaper, apparently obtained from a French source, as a backdrop for his American furniture in the rococo and Chinese taste: rare Philadelphia upholstered armchairs with fret-carved legs; tea tables with pierced galleries; a unique Williamsburg, Virginia, kettle stand with fret carving; and even three side chairs (which he believed were from Philadelphia) with carved crest-rails in the form of a pagoda.[41] He even initially placed his nest of Chinese lacquered tables in this parlor, but eventually moved them to his Imlay Room with the American painted furniture. The Chinese Parlor was an exquisitely colorful room, for which he selected the perfect shade of antique green silk damask for the curtains and slipcovers. However, he was quite aware of the fragile nature of this fabric, which could probably never be replaced, for he wrote his executors:

*I consider that I have been quite unselfish in not using during my lifetime the green damask curtains and the special matching slip seats in the Chinese wallpaper room. We all, including Mrs. Benkard, had one glorious day of enjoyment, and I think the directors agree that the color of the green damask must have been made especially for the wallpaper.*[42]

In 1958 du Pont purchased and installed in the Chinese Parlor one of his rarest and most unique tea tables (fig. 15).[43] Called a china table in the eighteenth century, this Newport example attributed to John Townsend (1733–1809) echoes Chinese design in the incised cross-hatching across the lower edge of the skirt, the pierced brackets, and especially the pierced cross-stretcher. The rococo-style pierced gallery surrounds the top and gives this form its name, for a ceramic tea set would be used atop the table. Though this is the only surviving Newport china table of this form known today, the 1792 inventory of Christopher Townsend, John's father, lists three china tables: two called "old blacknut" were relatively low in value, while the third, noted as "1 mahog

china table 10/," might well have resembled the Newport example.[44] This table is shown here under an English looking glass (fig. 15) whose gilt frame (with the possible exception of a great bedstead with a pagoda-like top for a canopy) comes closest to the fantasy and fancy that many designers of the period attempted to achieve in their expressions of the Chinese taste. Designed to be hung on a chimneybreast above a mantel, the carved frame combines elements of both Chinese and rococo taste in an engaging, almost whimsical manner. The maker of this looking glass might have derived inspiration from a number of designs for china cases, hanging shelves for china, and pier glass frames in Chippendale's 1762 edition of *The Gentleman and Cabinet-Maker's Director.*

Shimmering Chinese porcelains, like those atop the Newport table, were greatly coveted in the West. The Chinese had been producing high-fired, hard-paste porcelain reputedly since the middle of the T'ang dynasty (618–906); theirs was a country rich in the necessary raw materials—china stone (*petuntse*) and china clay (*kaolin*). Some of these porcelains reached the West with Marco Polo in the thirteenth century, and it was the Italians who christened these hard, shiny wares *porselaine,* which was derived from the word *porcellana* for the hard-bodied cowrie shell that resembled the body, back, and snout of a pig (*porcelana*). By the second half of the eighteenth century and the early nineteenth century, the Chinese, who carried on an extensive trade in paintings, produced for Western consumption illustrations of the production of their various exports, including tea and porcelain. The illustrated watercolors (figs. 16, 17) are part of a series

**16, 17** | *Digging the Ground for Porcelain*, China, 1800–1810; *Loading Boats for Canton*, China, 1800–1810 | These Chinese watercolors are part of a remarkable series that portrays with extraordinary detail the process and products of manufacturing and marketing porcelain for export.

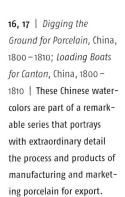

**18** | Punch bowl, England, 1735–1755; Bowl, Jingdezhen, China, 1710–1740 | In an effort to be both fashionable and competitive, English delftware manufacturers produced wares (such as the bowl on the left) that imitated expensive Chinese porcelains (such as the more diminutive bowl on the right, which might have been part of a tea set).

of twenty-three pictures detailing the entire process of this porcelain trade, from the digging of the raw clay (left), through the potting, firing, and painting, to the transporting of wares to Canton (right), where they were sold and shipped out. Although the Chinese presented a somewhat imaginary, romanticized view of this entire process (omitting any of the filth and pollution that were also produced), this series of illustrations is enormously informative.

Quantities of porcelain produced for export made their way to Europe and England after the founding of the Dutch and English East India Companies in the early seventeenth century. More limited quantities came to colonial America, as evidenced by the excavated shards of seventeenth-century blue-and-white Chinese porcelains found at several early settlement sites. The Chinese wares imported to Europe and England served as an inspiration for delftware (tin-glazed earthenware) and eventually for saltglazed white stoneware, as manufactories made wares both in direct imitation and with designs reminiscent of Chinese images and scenes. For example, a very small bowl (fig. 18, right) is typical of Chinese export wares of the first quarter of the eighteenth century. It was no accident that an English delftware manufactory, probably in London or Bristol, made larger bowls (fig. 18, left) almost directly copying the simple blue-and-white flora and fauna motifs. Even more interesting, this English delftware bowl (1735–1755) was owned by the Wendell family of Albany, New York, proving that even if only limited quantities of Chinese wares came to the colonies, European wares inspired by Chinese designs were available and probably cheaper.

Prior to the American Revolution, colonial access to the China trade market was for the most part controlled by the English. While those abroad could order enormous sets of dinnerwares from China, complete with individual monograms or elaborately painted coats of arms with crests, only a few wealthy colonials could, with connections, successfully procure the same wares. For instance, in 1747 Samuel Vaughan, an affluent Jamaican planter and merchant, married Sarah Hallowell of Boston; presumably soon after their union, Vaughan ordered via a London agent a handsome set of Chinese porcelain dinnerware. Ornamented with a combination of rococo and Chinese taste, the octagonal plates (fig. 19) were painted in black enamel with the arms of Vaughan impaling Hallowell (left half Vaughan, right half Hallowell) in a highly ornate, asymmetrical foliate surround with "Samuel Vaughan" written in script beneath. Around the rim, also painted in black, are four Chinese landscape views in scrolled surrounds of gold and red. This elegant dinner service must have made quite a splendid table in America, since very few colonials had such remarkable imported Chinese porcelain. How could Chinese painters reproduce so exactly these intricate coats of arms, whether for colonial, English, or European dinnerwares? Clients must have sent via the captain or supercargo an engraved impression of the arms they wanted painted on the dinner service. Presumably the most expedient way to do this was to send along an engraved bookplate, such as the one Samuel Vaughan owned and must have sent to China (fig. 20).

Samuel Shaw, the supercargo on the *Empress of China*'s 1784/1785 voyage bound for Canton, included in his journal descriptions detailing the system of purchasing and trading with the Chinese. Once the ship reached Whampoa at the mouth of the Pearl River in China, Shaw wrote:

*The supercargoes are provided with elegant factories* [hongs], *and every accommodation they can wish.... The factories at Canton, occupying less than a quarter of a mile in front, are situated on the bank of the river. The quay is enclosed by a rail-fence, which has stairs and a gate opening from the water to each factory, where all merchandise is received and sent away. The limits of the Europeans are extremely confined; there being, besides the quay, only a few streets in the suburbs, occupied by the trading people, which they are allowed to frequent. Europeans, after a dozen years' residence, have not seen more than what the first month presented to view. They are sometimes invited to dine with the Chinese merchants, who have houses and gardens on the opposite side of the river; but even then no new information is obtained. Everything of a domestic concern is strictly concealed.*[45]

Of the more costly "souvenirs" brought back to America were large porcelain punch bowls, now called Hong bowls, which depict the residences and trading posts (or *hongs*) of the supercargoes. Capt. John Green of the *Empress of China* purchased in 1784/1785

**19** | Plate, Jingdezhen, China, about 1755 | Porcelains ordered from China could be personalized; for instance, Samuel and Sarah Hallowell Vaughan bought a large set of dinnerware replete with their coat of arms.

**20** | Bookplate of Samuel Vaughan, probably England, 1747–1755 | Vaughan's arms must have been engraved sometime after his marriage to Sarah Hallowell of Boston in 1747, for this bookplate incorporates both the Vaughan and the Hallowell family coats of arms.

"4 Factory painted Bowles @ 5½ p—$22."[46] Presumably Green's bowls were somewhat similar to one (fig. 21) showing the rail-fence that enclosed the quay and the flags of the various nations trading at Canton. Limited numbers of these bowls, which were quite costly at the time, must have been imported by European and American traders. Not until about 1788 were Hong bowls displaying American flags produced. More plentiful and even more visually descriptive of the life and living quarters along the Pearl River at Canton were the numerous views of this lively and competitive business district (in 1757 the Chinese emperor confined all European trading to Canton). Oil paintings, watercolors, and gouaches on paper, pen and ink drawings, and reverse paintings on glass all provided a wide range of images of this populous port from about 1760 through the first half of the nineteenth century.[47] One painting (fig. 22) shows a very detailed view of the architecture of the *hongs,* with Westerners on second-floor balconies peering down to the bustling square, where a trial is about to begin.

Westerners purchased a wide range of items from the *hong* merchants at Canton. The bulk of exported goods consisted of tea and textiles, as well as paintings and portraits (large and miniature), hand-painted ivory fans, porcelain, silver and gold, carved jade and ivories, and lacquerwares and furniture made of bamboo and exotic woods in both Chinese and Western styles. Among the largest quantities of wares that came to American shores were enormous sets of porcelain for both tea and dinner. Packed and padded in baskets and boxes, these weighty wares formed a "floor" in the ship's

**21** | Hong punch bowl, China, 1788 – 1810 | The process of importing Chinese porcelains to America and Europe was a highly ritual-ized and restricted trade. As depicted on this punch bowl, each country estab-lished its own trading post along the Pearl River in Canton and marked its por-tion of the waterfront with its flag.

**22** | *View of the Foreign Factories in Canton*, China, 1800 – 1810 | *Hongs*, or trading posts, bustled with activity as European and American traders waited at the ports for their orders to be filled. Traders would rarely, if ever, be allowed to venture further into China than these ports, a restric-tion that added to the mys-tery of the trade.

**23** | Centerville stair hall | FitzHugh pattern porcelain, which typically includes a central medallion surrounded by four clusters of flowers and a complex border, was produced in China for the export market in a variety of colors, including green, orange, blue, and yellow.

**24** | Plate (detail), Jingdezhen, China, 1800–1820 | Chinese porcelains in the so-called FitzHugh pattern with a central motif of an eagle holding a ribbon inscribed "E Pluribus Unum" were popular with the American market after the Revolution. This device, essentially the great seal of the United States, was first adopted by Congress in 1782.

hull on which were packed more fragile goods that could not withstand the dampness in the hull. The most ordinary Chinese porcelains were painted in blue and white with Chinese scenes; they were referred to in period documents as either "Canton" or "Nanking," which denoted their place of export. The former was a more common ware, the latter, a better quality. Dinner services were particularly large, often numbering over 350 pieces ranging from dozens of plates, soup bowls, and platters, to covered vegetable dishes, covered soup tureens, sauceboats with under trays, and occasionally even a form as exotic as a condiment or curry set.[48] Wealthier Americans ordered services specially ornamented with their monogram in any number of different devices. Some more well-to-do Americans even owned more than one Chinese export dinner service: for instance, John Brown (1738–1803) of Providence, Rhode Island, ordered one set in 1789 (with his initials in a shield device), and a second service in 1795 (decorated with a distinctive floral urn).

Patriotic American insignia were also often emblazoned on wares for tea and dinner, including sets with sailing ships flying the American flag (see fig. 15). Some of the most impressive patriotic wares were those painted with great gilt eagles and brilliant green or orange decoration.[49] Patrons who commissioned such services often had their initial(s) placed on the shield on the eagle's breast. A cupboard filled with such patriotic porcelain (see figs. 23, 24) in the early years of the republic would have heralded not only the recently proclaimed independence of America, but also the new-found wealth of American entrepreneurs like Robert Morris, Elias Hasket Derby, and John Brown as they mined the resources of Canton and other ports of the East.

# 3. A Passion for Rococo

THE WIDELY POPULAR ROCOCO taste was a fashion that grew out of the baroque style in late seventeenth-century Italy; it was refined in France in the early eighteenth century and flourished throughout Europe in the first half of the eighteenth century. The word rococo probably derived from the French word *rocaille,* referring to the rocklike creations that ornamented fanciful grottoes of the late seventeenth and early eighteenth century. As manifest in architecture and decorative arts, this style embodied a wide range of naturalistic ornament, from shells to foliage and floral swags. Executed at its finest, it is exceedingly sculptural, flowing, and harmonious; the ornament becomes one with the form. From the Continent this style was taken to England by various emigré artisans in the 1720s and 1730s. Shortly before the middle of the century, its seeds sprouted in America, where it would come into full flower during the third quarter of the eighteenth century.

Knowledge of this fashion (and any style from abroad, for that matter) was carried across the ocean to the colonies in three primary ways: printed materials such as bookplates, trade advertisements, and catalogues, and published books on architecture, furniture designs, and various other drawings; actual objects made abroad and imported either by merchants for resale or by individual patrons for personal use; ideas carried in the minds of craftsmen who came to the colonies seeking greater economic freedom and opportunity, and ideas brought by patrons who had traveled abroad. One popular design book, London cabinetmaker Thomas Chippendale's *The Gentleman and Cabinet-*

*Maker's Director* (published first in 1754 with two subsequent editions in 1755 and 1762), was readily available in America. Chippendale was such a successful entrepreneur and promoter of the rococo that the style has become popularly known as the Chippendale style both abroad and in America. Ironically, artisans of the period complained that it was virtually impossible to execute most of his designs as drawn. Although numerous copies of Chippendale's publication were in colonial America, few designs were slavishly copied in the colonies.

One of Henry Francis du Pont's greatest collecting passions was Chippendale furniture and accompanying furnishings. In 1952 he reflected upon his love of this style, which he noted, "appealed to me for various reasons. It was sturdy and suitable for practical use. Also, I was interested in its many variations, not only within one type, such as Philadelphia chairs, but among the widely differing products of regions showing different influences—Boston, Newport, New York and Philadelphia."[1] Although in the early 1920s he had collected some Chippendale pieces for Chestertown House, his summer residence in Southampton, Long Island,[2] he did not collect high style, urban Chippendale furniture in earnest until later in that decade. In 1929 he was totally captivated, paying a record price, $44,000, at the New York auction sale of the collection of Howard Reifsnyder for a quintessential Chippendale piece: the famed Van Pelt-Turner family Philadelphia high chest.[3] By then, he had already begun a major addition to Winterthur, which he had inherited in 1927. At that time he had determined that the principal rooms in his country estate residence should be in the taste and style embraced by well-to-do colonists from coastal urban ports, principally Philadelphia, in the third quarter of the eighteenth century. He had already acquired woodwork "too sophisticated for the other rooms in the Southampton house,"[4] and before long he would assemble some of the finest examples of carved architectural interiors of the pre-Revolutionary period.

Among the finest expressions of rococo interior architectural ornament in America is the Stamper-Blackwell Parlor now installed at Winterthur (fig. 1). The parlor originally graced a Philadelphia house built in the early 1760s on Pine Street for merchant and one-time mayor John Stamper, and later owned by Rev. William Blackwell. It was in Philadelphia, by 1750 the largest and most economically successful colonial port city, that the Chippendale (or rococo) style achieved its fullest expression—indeed, the late baroque (or Queen Anne) style had also reached its zenith in that city. The money was there, the sophisticated taste was there, and because of these factors, the talent was there: English-trained carvers, cabinetmakers, and various other artisans flocked to this center literally to cash in on the opportunities. Many of the same craftsmen who were commissioned to execute elaborate interior woodwork were also called upon by cabinet-

**1** | Stamper-Blackwell Parlor | Henry Francis du Pont furnished this architecturally ornate pre-Revolutionary room appropriately with some of his most high-style furniture. Among these treasures are extremely rare pieces having hairy paw feet: the Charleston easy chair on the left and John Cadwalader's side chair and a Philadelphia fire screen on the right.

makers and chairmakers to embellish furniture. London-trained carvers such as Nicholas Bernard and Martin Jugiez, Hercules Courtney, and James Reynolds were key figures in the dissemination of this fashionable style to Philadelphia.

Although few pieces of eighteenth-century English furniture with American histories of ownership are recognized today, surviving documents leave no doubt that American and English production comingled in some of the finest colonial interiors of the period. Even more prevalent in America were luxury goods (like ceramics, glass, and textiles) that the colonists had neither been able to produce successfully, or cheaply enough, to be competitive with those made abroad and imported. Thus, the colonies were Great Britain's major market for both luxury goods and other items manufactured prior to the Revolution. Indeed, fabric of English manufacture found a ready market in America: in 1765 it was reported that approximately 90,616 yards were exported to the colonies; by 1785 that amount had grown to 353,762 yards.[5] These imports included sophisticated woven and printed textiles that present superb visual expressions of rococo taste. Winterthur's copperplate-printed cotton (fig. 2), manufactured in Surrey, England, about 1765–1775, displays all the curvilinear grace of the best and boldest rococo designs.

Naturalistic, abundant, and overdone, a panoply of fruits, flowers, and foliage entwine about a rustic trunk that spirals upward in a series of *S*-curves. A printed cotton such as this might have been used for bed or window hangings, or even loose cases (slipcovers) on furniture. Since the cost of copperplate-printed fabrics was probably based on the amount of engraved detail, this pattern must have been very expensive.

Another textile highly expressive of rococo taste (though also probably inspired by designs on imported Eastern goods from China and India) is Winterthur's English polychrome cotton (fig. 3) printed with exotic long-tailed birds, gnarled branches, and abundant blossoms. The scale of the design and the number of colors indicate that it is of superb quality. This type of print would also have been used in households for furnishing beds and windows, as well as for covering furniture with loose cases. This particular piece in Winterthur's extensive textile collection carries the same design found on a set of bed hangings owned by Maj. Gen. Edward Hand (1744–1802) and used at his home, Rock Ford, in Lancaster, Pennsylvania, where he moved in 1793.

By the eighteenth century, the entire world—comprising four diverse continents—was a boundless source of raw and manufactured materials to be traded and moved about for the pleasure and profit of a large community of tradesmen, merchants, and aristocrats. It is not surprising that by the middle of the century luxury items were made to celebrate this bountiful world and to acknowledge a patron's knowledge of and ability to possess objects from faraway places. The Derby China Works in England, for one, produced an extraordinary quartet of figures (fig. 4) representing the four continents: Europe, Asia, Africa, and America. Perhaps modeled after similar hard-paste figures produced at the Meissen porcelain factory in Germany, each of these imposing soft-paste porcelain figures stands just over a foot in height. With poses echoing the curvy, scroll-like forms seen in various other rococo objects, they are the epitome of rococo design. Standing on craggy, rocklike mounds, each figure is surrounded by the flora and fauna of its respective continent: Europe holds an orb in one hand and wears a crown on her head, while war trophies, fruit, flowers, and symbolic objects lie strewn at her feet; Asia holds a flaming urn and flowers, while a camel lies at her feet; Africa wears an elephant headdress and straddles a crouching lion; and America, garbed in native dress replete with a feather headdress, stands with one foot on a crocodile. Cesare Ripa's *Iconologia* (Rome, 1603) may have been the original inspiration for such figures.[6] The presence of English-made "china figures" in colonial households is well documented; they were usually found ornamenting mantelpieces and were sometimes moved onto the dining table to become part of a centerpiece during the service of dessert.[7]

2 | Plate-printed cotton (detail), Nixon & Company, Surrey, England, 1765–1775 | Nature, the key source of inspiration for rococo design, served as the model for this English copperplate-printed cotton. The twining trunk displays a variety of fruits, flowers, and foliage.

3 | Block-printed cotton (detail), England, 1775–1790 | This English printed cotton reflects the fashion for rococo designs of exotic naturalistic motifs. Most frequently used for bed and window hangings, such fabrics were also fashioned into slipcovers for upholstered furniture.

**4 |** "The Four Continents," Derby, England, 1760–1770 | Fascination with exploration and discovery, the exotic and the wild, inspired porcelain manufacturers to produce fanciful figures such as these for a burgeoning market in luxury products.

Although England did not encourage the colonies to compete with its own manufacturers of certain luxury goods, such as stylish ceramics, glass, textiles, and brass, it seemed to have no problem with colonial production of utilitarian pottery, glass, and iron. America supplied England with pig iron (ingots of iron), which was made into such fashionable products as coal grates. However, colonists (who heated with wood, unlike the English, who predominantly used coal) were apparently allowed to produce objects necessary for heating, such as chimneybacks (firebacks), stoves, and andirons. A ready and boundless American supply of the necessary raw materials—iron ore, limestone, wood, and water power—enabled the colonists to manufacture these utilitarian objects locally. Although many of these products were exceedingly plain and unornamented, some were fashionably embellished, copying similar imported objects that introduced new styles to the colonies. A monumental cast-iron chimneyback (fig. 5) with the British royal arms is such an example, either copying a similar chimneyback imported from England or copying the device from other forms, such as the carved and painted wood arms that ornamented the pew in Christ Church, Philadelphia, when the governor of Pennsylvania worshiped there.[8] Cast at the Oxford Furnace in Warren County, New Jersey, and dated 1747 across the bottom, this colonial chimneyback is decorated with design elements that announce the impending rococo

5 | Chimneyback, Oxford Furnace, Warren County, New Jersey, 1747 | This cast-iron chimneyback depicting the British royal arms echoes the European taste for the rococo style that would soon captivate America.

6 | Chimneyback, Aetna Furnace, Burlington County, New Jersey, 1770 – 1774 | The leaping stag depicted on this chimneyback recalls the hunt, an age-old ritual signifying wealth and aristocracy. The stag's gracefully arched neck echoes the flowing scrolls, both of which express the rococo fashion.

style. The boldly sculptural acanthus leaves that flank the crowned helmet at the top, combined with the repetition of scrolled motifs, are evocative of the style as it was just beginning to become all the rage in the colonies. The molds for these sand-cast chimneybacks were usually carved of mahogany by skilled craftsmen who also produced carving for architectural interiors and furniture.[9]

An interesting comparison to the Oxford Furnace chimneyback is one made between 1770 and 1774 at the height of the rococo taste in America, on the eve of the Revolution, at the Aetna Furnace in Burlington County, New Jersey, just east of Philadelphia (fig. 6). Similar in overall proportion and shape to the Oxford Furnace chimneyback (fig. 5), the Aetna Furnace example features a leaping stag. A recurring motif in various media during the rococo period, the stag evokes the "hunt," a pastime of the aristocracy and hence symbolic of position and wealth. This same leaping stag is repeated on chimneybacks made in New England and retailed in Boston by merchant Joseph Webb from the late 1760s through the early 1780s.[10] However, the Aetna piece, with its addition of foliate scrolls and its overall looser, more flowing aspect, is much more closely derivative of rococo ornament. As has been noted by other scholars of the American rococo, "in both composition and carving, the ornamental design bears a strong resemblance to the tympanum boards of some Philadelphia case furniture."[11] It is not surprising that this New Jersey furnace produced exceedingly sophisticated and fashionable ironwork, for its founder Charles Read, the offspring of a successful Philadelphia mercantile family, was certainly familiar with the stylish rococo taste.

While fashion-conscious consumers carefully protected the brick of their fireplaces with handsomely ornamented cast-iron chimneybacks, they also enhanced their overmantels (or chimneybreasts) with portraits, scenic paintings, and occasionally a needlework landscape done by a young lady of the household. Just as chimneybacks, and numerous other objects made in the colonies, took their inspiration from precedents produced across the pond, so too did needlework pictures.[12] Often framed as overmantel looking glasses were (replete with brass sconces on either side for candles), these colorful, complex pieces were worked on a very fine linen canvas; hence, in the period they were called canvaswork. Evocative of the pastoral, naturalistic imagery and symbolism of the rococo taste, these pieces had their direct sources in English engraved prints as well as in English overmantel canvaswork pieces. A growing body of related works dubbed fishing-lady canvaswork pictures has been identified by needlework scholars since the first quarter of the twentieth century. Similar motifs, from figures to flora and fauna, reverberate throughout these bucolic landscapes: graceful ladies fishing, shepherdesses reclining, gentlemen suitors conversing, hounds and huntsmen, and leaping stags. The leaping stags of these canvaswork pieces bear a striking resemblance to those seen on rococo chimneybacks, yet the canvas pieces exhibit a fuller depiction of the hunt scene.

Winterthur's collection includes a remarkable fishing-lady overmantel (fig. 7) dating from 1748. While attending boarding school in Boston, eighteen-year-old Sarah Warren (1730–1797) worked this piece (possibly as a final masterwork), marking the culmination of her schooling. Born and raised in Barnstable, Massachusetts (on Cape Cod), Sarah was one of many young women (and men) from prosperous, educated families who were sent to urban centers such as Boston for their education. And Sarah was not the only Barnstable girl to go to school in Boston and to produce such a laudable masterwork; two other girls from the same town, Eunice Bourne and Hannah Otis (both two years Sarah's junior), probably attended the same school.[13] And Eunice's canvaswork overmantel, also dated 1748, is so similar to Sarah's that the two pieces may well have been directed by the same teacher and copied from the same source.[14] Hannah and Sarah were eventually related by marriage. Both girls' brothers (each named James) were at Harvard in the early 1740s, along with another young man, William Sever (1729–1809) of Kingston, Massachusetts (a town near Plymouth just about halfway between Boston and Barnstable). In 1754 James Warren married Mercy Otis, Hannah's older sister (who must also have been schooled in Boston), and in 1755 Sarah married William Sever. Remarkably, Sarah Warren Sever's canvaswork chimneypiece remained in the possession of her descendants (who had kept it in the house in Kingston built about 1755 by William Sever) until acquired by du Pont in 1941.

**7** | Needlework picture, Sarah Warren, Boston, 1748 | The fishing lady in the center of Sarah Warren's canvaswork links it to a group of similar pictures worked by young ladies attending Boston schools during the mid-eighteenth century. The original frame with brass fittings for sconces suggests this piece would have hung over a fireplace.

Only rarely do groups of valued possessions descend through a family and enter intact the collections of a museum where they continue to tell the story of the people who acquired and owned them. Fortunately, this is the case with a number of important objects owned by William and Sarah Warren Sever. In addition to Sarah's fine canvaswork overmantel picture, du Pont in 1941 acquired from Sever's descendants an unusual Boston tea table, along with the Chinese porcelain tea wares that presumably were often used on it (fig. 8). This tea table, with its twelve semicircular projections, might simply have been called a square tea table when it was made soon after the Severs married in 1755. Scholars and collectors today describe it as a turret-top, or scallop-top, tea table. The form was produced only in Boston and may be a uniquely American variation (only five American examples are known today) on English circular, scallop-top examples.[15] Related to earlier Boston round or turret-cornered card tables, these highly sophisticated examples must have been exceedingly costly, with their molded rim carved from the solid mahogany top. The Severs' mansion house in Kingston was a large, square Georgian house with sophisticated interior woodwork, extensive grounds and gardens, and no doubt rich and expensive furnishings.[16] Interestingly, Sarah Warren Sever's sister-in-law Mercy Otis Warren (a noted poet and author) owned a related but unique trefoil-lobed kettle stand, as well as a turret-cornered card table for which she made an elaborate canvaswork top depicting playing cards and mother-of-pearl counters.[17] It is not difficult to imagine that Mercy also had a turret-top tea table, and that Sarah's table and Mercy's kettle stand and card table came from the same shop.

**8** | Tea table, Boston, 1755–1765; Assembled tea set, China, 1730–1770; Candlesticks, John Burt, Boston, about 1720 | Sarah Warren used this table and china to serve tea, a social ritual in the mid-eighteenth century. An intriguing form peculiar to Boston, the turret-top tea table has semicircular projections no doubt designed to perfectly fit a cup and saucer.

Although the Severs' tea table is in the rococo taste, with its turrets, asymmetrical foliate carving on the knees of its cabriole legs, and claw-and-ball feet, this Boston interpretation of the style is quite different from what was simultaneously happening in New York; Philadelphia; Williamsburg, Virginia; and Charleston, South Carolina. Why was this the case, when Thomas Chippendale had just published the first edition of *The Gentleman and Cabinet-Maker's Director* and the height of rococo taste was already being exhibited in Philadelphia? Here, as everywhere else in life, economics rules. Boston reached its zenith economically by the 1730s, after which time the balance of population and power began to shift slowly toward New York and Philadelphia.

By midcentury, Philadelphia was the largest mercantile center in the colonies. What did this mean and how did it affect the regional accents of various useful, yet decorative, arts made in these major urban centers? Simply speaking, emigré craftsmen from abroad, especially London, gravitated to the urban center with the greatest wealth, bringing with them the most fashionable taste. Because Boston did not experience the influx of emigré English, Scottish, and Irish artisans that Philadelphia did, the taste of Boston patrons and the production of local craftsmen were quite different, seemingly more restrained, and perhaps more provincial than the high style rococo taste manifest in Philadelphia. Nevertheless, the importation of English furniture into Boston during the eighteenth century had an impact on the taste of elite patrons and hence on the production of Boston cabinetmakers. Specific carving motifs and English forms such as double chairback settees and bombé case furniture were almost exclusively adopted in that center because of the influence of imported examples. Wealthy Boston merchant Charles Apthorp (1698–1758) owned a monumental English mahogany clothespress with bombé base and mirrored doors in the upper case.[18] When he died in 1758, his estate inventory taken the following year listed "a Mohogony Beauro with Glass doors…£32:00:00" in the "Great Parlour," and "a Mohogony Cabinet with glass doors…£30:00:00" in the "Dining Room up Stairs." Perhaps based on Apthorp's example or other English bombé cases owned in that city, Boston patrons developed a proclivity for this form, and cabinetmakers mastered its unusual aspects in the construction of chests of drawers, chest-on-chests, desks, and desks and bookcases. Costly and emblematic of position and wealth, the bombé form became the choice of a small and elite Boston mercantile society.

Although closely related to other bombé case furniture, Winterthur's desk and bookcase (fig. 9) is extraordinary and distinct from any other known examples. While the lower section resembles other Boston desks and chests with its serpentine front, blocked ends, and short cabriole legs with claw-and-ball feet, the upper section is unlike any other Boston case furniture. Strongly dependent on English designs, its form and ornament are closely derived from several plates (nos. 51, 64, 94) published by the Society of Upholsterers' in *The II d Edition of Genteel Houshold Furniture In the Present Taste* (London, 1764 or 1765)[19] (fig. 10). The design and carving of this upper section presents a more dominant rococo taste than is evidenced on most other Boston case furniture of the second half of the eighteenth century. Was the choice of this design dictated by the patron who ordered it (presumably merchant Edward Brinley, 1730–1809) or by the maker (probably John Cogswell, 1738–1819)? Might one of these gentlemen have owned a copy of this useful book on designs for "Houshold Furniture"? It has been suggested that with a new generation of mercantile elite emerging by the end of the Revolution,

**9** | Desk and bookcase, Boston, 1780 – 1795 | A rare combination of typical Boston features on the desk and English-inspired rococo elements on the bookcase makes this unusual and costly piece a fine example of how European and British designs were selectively melded to create uniquely American expressions.

**10** | Plate 51, from *The II^d Edition of Genteel Houshold Furniture In the Present Taste* (London, 1764 or 1765) | This plate was one of the sources for the upper case of a Boston desk and bookcase (fig. 9). Although whether or not the patron or cabinetmaker possessed this London design book is not known, it undoubtedly was owned in Boston in the second half of the eighteenth century.

**11** | *The Gore Children*, John Singleton Copley, Boston, about 1755 | Group portraits of children were rare in eighteenth-century America, but seventeen-year-old John Singleton Copley was undaunted by the challenge. His accomplished painting heralded the beginning of a brilliant career in colonial America.

"society as a whole became more cosmopolitan and more receptive to new ideas and stylistic influences."[20] While cabinetmakers like Cogswell could satisfy the demands of conservative patrons, who preferred traditional bombé furniture based on late baroque English examples, he could also meet the tastes "of more progressive clients who wanted commode facades, sculptural ornaments, and rococo carving derived from English design books."[21] The one area in which Bostonians most fully embraced the rococo style was in the elaborately carved original frames found on many portraits by the Boston-born painter John Singleton Copley (1738-1815).[22]

Copley grew up in Boston, training under his stepfather Peter Pelham, an engraver. In 1755 (when William Sever married Sarah Warren), the seventeen-year-old artist took on an ambitious group portrait of four (of the thirteen) children of John and Frances Pinckney Gore (fig. 11). How could Gore, a coach painter who was not part of the wealthier mercantile community, afford such a seemingly costly purchase? And why (if he wanted images of his children—not an easy task given their young ages) did he ask a relatively unknown young artist to attempt this challenging commission? Gore certainly did not have an extensive choice of artists: Robert Feke and John Smibert had died and John Greenwood had gone to Surinam, leaving only native-born artist Joseph Badger, who was not exactly a leading light. Joseph Blackburn, the English portrait artist, had probably not yet arrived in Boston, but even if he had, Gore would probably

not have been able to afford him, for a coach painter's pocketbook could not have been large. It is documented that Gore did business with Copley, and perhaps a barter agreement between them afforded Gore a reasonable price and Copley some painting supplies in exchange for the work.[23] Furthermore, the challenge of this complex commission gave Copley the opportunity to show his talents, perhaps even to some of Gore's prominent patrons. Reminiscent of conventions and poses seen in both Smibert's and Feke's work, which was certainly known by the youthful Copley, the Gore painting represents a worthy effort and demonstrates the artist's latent talent, which would be further challenged in the ensuing years.[24]

Almost three hundred miles south of Boston, in Philadelphia, the aesthetic climate was quite different. Thomas Chippendale's *The Gentleman and Cabinet-Maker's Director* was such an influential publication that on the eve of the Revolution an American edition was being prepared by a Philadelphia printer, but the outbreak of war halted this effort.[25] Just a cursory review of the production of Philadelphia artisans compared with that of Boston clearly demonstrates that a more English-based rococo taste was embraced by the elite in Philadelphia. As the largest urban port in the colonies, Philadelphia was the center of wealth and sophisticated taste. In addition to its native-born artisans, its circumstance attracted numerous talents trained abroad. For the most part, it was these craftsmen who brought rococo style and taste to the city and heightened the quality of ornament executed on everything from interior woodwork to furniture. To compete with English porcelain imports, two entrepreneurial gentlemen, Gousse Bonnin and George Anthony Morris, established a porcelain manufactory in 1770. Unfortunately, confronted with technical difficulties, costs, and competition from abroad, the company ceased production before the end of 1772.[26]

Imported luxury objects, such as cast brass sconces (see detail of fig. 12) and an impressive English earthenware, four-tier Grand Platt Menage atop a card table (fig. 12), no doubt helped to disseminate the rococo style in American urban centers, especially Philadelphia.[27] Probably ordered by retailers from printed catalogues distributed by English manufacturers, these wares may have served as inspiration for craftsmen working in other media. One of the finest, most important examples of this phenomenon, a carved and painted looking glass (fig. 12) made for the house of John Cadwalader on Second Street in 1770–1771, was probably carved by James Reynolds.[28] Surviving bills document Cadwalader's purchase of six looking glasses from Reynolds in 1770–1771; three were "carv'd & burnish gold," two were "party [partial] gold," and one was "in a Carv'd white frame."[29] This "white frame" very likely describes the frame now at Winterthur, given the dimensions in the bill (which closely match the Winterthur frame)

**12** | Sconces, London or Birmingham, England, 1760–1780; Card table, Philadelphia, 1765–1780; Looking glass, attributed to James Reynolds, Philadelphia, 1770–1771; Grand Platt Menage, Staffordshire or Yorkshire, England, 1775–1810 | Elite Philadelphians, such as John Cadwalader (who owned the Reynolds looking glass), expressed their approbation of the rococo style through the acquisition of opulent and ornate possessions. Stunning English- and American-made objects such as these ornamented their homes and signaled both their taste and wealth. The arabesque sconce (see detail opposite), with its foliate candle cup and asymmetrical foliate cartouche, derives its inspiration from French rococo designs of the mid-eighteenth century. It numbers among the many English brass sconces that were imported into America during the third quarter of the eighteenth century.

and a recent finish analysis (what was called white at that time was more likely a stone color). Few American objects express the rococo as fully as does this frame, which is almost entirely composed of intersecting *C*-scrolls and *S*-scrolls embellished with foliage and trailing floral sprays; these elements are echoed in the movement and motifs seen in the imported brass sconces and earthenware centerpiece.

The card table beneath the looking glass presents Philadelphia rococo furniture in a most understated yet superbly executed manifestation. Exquisitely proportioned and balanced, this table exemplifies how ornament can become one with form in seamless harmony. The delicate foliate scrolls gently roll across the lower edge of the skirt in much the same manner as the scrolls of the looking glass ornament its edges. The carved foliage trails down the curved knees of the cabriole legs in typical Philadelphia style. The serpentine shape of the top, with its molded edge and projecting corners, echoes the movement of the skirt and the swelling of the cabriole legs. Although not the most elaborately embellished Philadelphia rococo card table, this example is certainly one of the most successful.

The most elaborate rococo furniture made in eighteenth-century America was undoubtedly owned by the Cadwaladers.[30] In 1768 John Cadwalader (already a gentleman of significant means, given the great wealth of his mother's family, the Lamberts) married Elizabeth Lloyd, daughter of one of the largest and wealthiest landowners in Maryland, Edward Lloyd III of Talbot County. Elizabeth brought a sizable dowry to this union. By 1769, knowing that the young couple wished to acquire a town house in Philadelphia, Lloyd had advanced his daughter some of her inheritance. The Cadwaladers purchased a brick house on Second Street. Though substantial (38 × 41 ft., three stories high), it was simply appointed. Within two years this dwelling underwent renovation and major embellishment by the city's most notable craftsmen, including Benjamin Randolph, Nicholas Bernard and Martin Jugiez, Hercules Courtney, and James Reynolds. Indeed the interior woodwork probably surpassed that of the Stamper-Blackwell House (see fig. 1) built about the same time on Pine Street. Elaborate architectural carving, stucco and plasterwork ceilings, gilt papier-mâché borders, and costly window hangings and upholstery fabrics were all part of this extraordinary array of taste and wealth. But the denouement of the Cadwalader's display, much of which survives today as visible evidence, was the exquisitely carved furniture: side chairs, pole screens, an easy chair, card tables, slab tables, and looking glasses.

To this day, the Cadwalader's side chairs (fig. 13) are among the most coveted prizes for American collectors of eighteenth-century Philadelphia furniture. The same craftsmen

**13** | Side chair, attributed to shop of Thomas Affleck, Philadelphia, 1770 | This chair is one of seven that survive from a larger set of ribband-back chairs ordered by John Cadwalader for his Philadelphia town house in 1770. The cabinetmaker, presumably Thomas Affleck, may have fashioned the chairs by using a design from Thomas Chippendale's *Director* (fig. 14) or, perhaps, by using actual English chairs owned in Philadelphia.

who executed the carved architectural work of the house also ornamented the furniture, assuring a sense of visual unity throughout. Surviving bills and receipts document much of this work, though clearly this information is not complete. Consequently, scholars today must simply attribute the seven surviving ribband-back side chairs with saddle seats and upholstery half over the rails to the shop of Thomas Affleck (1740–1795). A Scottish-born Quaker who arrived in Philadelphia in 1763, Affleck had apprenticed in Edinburgh and worked in London prior to his arrival in America. While a surviving bill from Affleck for £119. 8 documents furniture made for the Cadwaladers between mid-October 1770 and mid-January 1771 (with additional charges of £61.4 for carving by Reynolds and Bernard and Jugiez), the ribband-back side chairs do not appear in that listing and were probably part of a separate billing. No doubt conversant with the most fashionable London styles and familiar with (if not in possession of) Chippendale's *Director,* Affleck would have been the obvious choice to execute the most elaborate furniture for the front parlor. Whether Affleck suggested the exact design or the Cad-

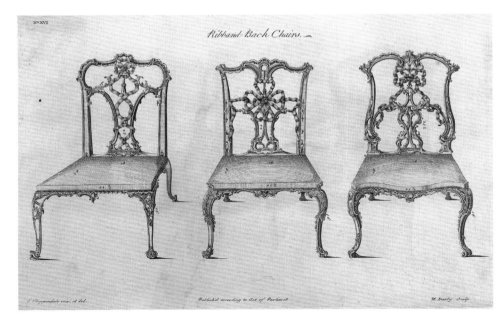

**14** | Plate 16, from *The Gentleman and Cabinet-Maker's Director*, Thomas Chippendale (London, 1754) | When producing furniture for their patrons, Philadelphia cabinetmakers often found inspiration in Thomas Chippendale's design book. A set of chairs (fig. 13) attributed to Thomas Affleck and made for John Cadwalader of Philadelphia was very likely based on the design shown here.

waladers themselves chose the ribband-back form directly from a plate in the *Director* (fig. 14) or from similar English chairs they may have seen in Philadelphia is not known. Another significant, and more costly, feature distinguished all of this furniture: the fully carved, hairy paw feet. Denoting a more stylish design, these feet closely followed the Chippendale example, for nowhere in the *Director* are claw-and-ball feet illustrated; French scroll feet, hairy paw feet, and Marlborough legs were the prevailing preferences. No doubt the Cadwaladers wanted more elegant furnishings that would be distinguished from others in the city, and they succeeded.

Just as the Cadwaladers' home was completed and they moved in with their new furnishings, they commissioned five large portraits of their family to grace the walls of their first-floor parlors.[31] And they chose the most noted local painter at the time, Charles Willson Peale (1741–1827), who just the year before, in the spring of 1771, had gone to Maryland to paint four works (two miniatures and two large canvases) for Edward Lloyd IV (1744–1796), Elizabeth Lloyd Cadwalader's brother. Equally as wealthy as the Cadwaladers, Lloyd and his wife, the former Elizabeth Tayloe (daughter of Gen. John Tayloe of Mount Airy, near Warsaw, Richmond County, Virginia), were depicted by Peale with their daughter Anne in a monumental canvas (fig. 15). Fully representing the gentility, position, and wealth that the Lloyds possessed, this portrait shows them richly attired and in poses symbolic of their accomplishments: Elizabeth, as a gentlewoman, plays an English guitar; and Edward, as a gentleman (of considerable size), assumes a posture suggesting ease and leisure. Peale only painted five large

**15** | *The Edward Lloyd Family,* Charles Willson Peale, Maryland, 1771 | Edward Lloyd, one of the wealthiest men in Maryland, is depicted with his wife Elizabeth Tayloe and their first child, Anne, four years after the couple's marriage. The portrait distinctly conveys the wealth and prominence of the family, who lived at Wye House in Talbot County, as well as endearing aspects of their lives: young Anne pulls her skirt back to reveal a pink petticoat as her father gently holds her other hand.

**16** | (Overleaf) Port Royal Parlor | Du Pont's eye for balance and symmetry is perhaps nowhere more evident than in his brilliant assemblage of rococo furniture in the parlor from Port Royal. Almost double its original size in order to accommodate both du Pont's collection and twentieth-century lifestyle, the parlor (installed at Winterthur between 1929 and 1931) nevertheless evokes the richness of Philadelphia's finest eighteenth-century production.

family group portraits (two of which were the Lloyds and the Cadwaladers; two others depicted the artist's own family), suggesting that such commissions were exceedingly costly, and therefore only the very wealthiest could afford them.[32]

By acquiring many of the same types of furniture and furnishings that were owned by families such as the Cadwaladers and the Lloyds, Henry Francis du Pont was able to create several period rooms that he believed evoked the eighteenth century. His impressive Port Royal Parlor (fig. 16)—sometimes called the most beautiful room in America —was for him perhaps the equivalent of the Cadwaladers' great double parlor. Using woodwork—though not nearly as highly ornamented as the Cadwaladers'—purchased from Port Royal (fig. 17), a large Georgian country house built about 1762 along Frankford Creek, north of Philadelphia, du Pont embellished the main entrance hall and principal parlor for his country house estate. Because of the dimensions of the wing he added and because he desired a very large room, the size of this space is almost twice that of the original parlor at Port Royal. Although du Pont attempted, in his words, "to show America as it had been,"[33] he essentially created colonial revival interiors. Although period rooms at Winterthur, like the Port Royal Parlor, are furnished with objects from the colonies, du Pont also appointed them with some objects that might not have been in colonial America. Most of his rooms he overambitiously furnished, but that

is what makes them such fascinating colonial revival period pieces. His obsession with color harmony, symmetry, textiles, floral arrangements, and placement resulted in rooms that resonated with perhaps a fuller tone than they would have in the eighteenth century. Acquiring and using antique fabrics whenever he could for window hangings and upholstery, du Pont implemented four seasonal changes a year for every room. These changes were planned to harmonize the colors of his interiors with his exterior spaces, or gardens, where nature's glories (or his own carefully orchestrated plantings) were transformed with the seasons.

Du Pont filled the Port Royal Parlor with some of his most glorious and impressive Philadelphia Chippendale furniture, reserving his eight pieces of Cadwalader furniture for the more appropriately proportioned and ornamented Stamper-Blackwell Parlor (see fig. 1) that adjoins the Port Royal room.[34] Always bearing in mind symmetry and balance, du Pont flanked the fireplace with two pieces that had descended in the Dickinson family: a rare pair of cabriole leg sofas with claw-and-ball feet. On either side of the chimneybreast, he arranged matching marbletop pier tables with applied foliate carving across their skirts. Opposite the fireplace, on the north wall between the doors leading to the main Port Royal Entrance Hall, du Pont placed a towering Philadelphia desk and bookcase with a pierced, latticework pediment.[35] The east and west walls, behind each of the sofas, provided a broad pier between two windows, the perfect setting for impressive, pedimented high chests. Both of these high chests are among his most prized Philadelphia case furniture: the famed Van Pelt highboy (introduction, fig. 5) on the west wall and the Gratz family high chest (see fig. 16) on the east wall.

The boldest and most monumental high chest at Winterthur is the Philadelphia piece (fig. 18) made for Michael and Miriam Simon Gratz, presumably just prior to or soon after their marriage in 1769. Gratz, a Jewish merchant originally from Langendorff, Silesia (today Poland), had apprenticed in London and in mid-1759 moved to Philadelphia, following his brother Barnard, who had emigrated in 1754. Upon his arrival, Michael Gratz took over his brother's position as a clerk in the mercantile firm of Levy and Franks, but by 1768 he and Barnard had formed their own business, B. and M. Gratz, Merchants.[36] By the time of his marriage to Miriam Simon, the daughter of one of Lancaster's most affluent and prominent Jewish merchants, he was on his way to acquiring considerable wealth through coastal and sea trade. A member of Philadelphia's large, prosperous Jewish community and of the congregation Mikveh Israel, Michael Gratz must have lived in a relatively lavish style. Even as a young lad working in London in his late teens, he was called an English nabob by family members for apparently spending his profits on sartorial finery.[37]

**17** | Port Royal, near Philadelphia, built about 1762 | This great Georgian country house built along Frankfurt Creek, north of Philadelphia, is among the most significant pre-Revolutionary homes that survived into the twentieth century. The classical proportions and symmetry (marking both the exterior and interior) doubtless attracted du Pont, who acquired interior woodwork from it in 1928.

**18** | High chest, Philadelphia, 1760 – 1770 | Deliberately showy aptly describes Miriam and Michael Gratz' extraordinary furniture, especially this remarkable mahogany high chest. The original cartouche, superior carving across the tympanum and skirt, and the imported chinoiserie brass hardware are testimony to both the artistry and expense of the piece.

**19** | Dressing table, Philadelphia, 1760–1770; Side chair, Philadelphia, 1760–1770 | Matching carved ornamentation clearly indicates that the Gratzes ordered a set of chairs to complement their brilliantly conceived case furniture—the dressing table shown here and their high chest (fig. 18). Such en suite sets were rare in pre-Revolutionary furnishing schemes.

The features that made the Gratz high chest a most costly item when it was constructed also distinguish it today as a superlative object: the massively carved, original cartouche (topmost ornament above the pediment); the carved rosettes and abundance of carved, applied foliate ornament and the freestanding shell in the tympanum (the space beneath the broken scroll pediment); the engaged fluted columns in the upper case and the vine-carved columns in the lower case; the heavily carved skirt; and the fully carved cabriole legs. Another factor that speaks to the high cost of this piece is the superior quality, highly figured mahogany that was carefully selected and effectively used on the drawer fronts. The ultimate punctuation on the façade is carried out through the use of the most elaborate and expensive form of brasses: ornate, Chinese style, and coated with a tinted lacquer to appear as if they were actually gilded. Patrons such as Michael Gratz frequently ordered dressing tables (fig. 19) to accompany high chests. However, the brasses, which are original on both the Gratz high chest and dressing table, are not the same pattern, and a close examination of the carving and construction on both pieces suggests that they may not have been made in the same cabinet shop. This discrepancy in brasses and techniques suggests that these case pieces were ordered at different times. The Gratzes also owned a set of side chairs that were made to match their high chest and dressing table. The asymmetrical, pendant shell carved in the front rail of the side chair (fig. 19) is similar in design and execution to those in the lower cases of the high chest and dressing table. While a few other instances of seating furniture made en suite with case furniture are known, such sets were a relatively rare occurrence in eighteenth-century America.

The introduction of new styles, or ornament indicative of a new style, is frequently manifest first in smaller imported objects such as ceramics or metalwork. For instance, London-made silver might introduce a style to the colonies even before engraved design sources or pieces of furniture in the new taste arrived. Once a new-fashioned object is available or in use, the likelihood of its being copied by enterprising artisans is almost certain. Such circumstances may well have led up to the Boston silversmith Thomas Edwards' (1701/1702–1755) being commissioned to make an ornate salver (fig. 20) about 1750. The elaborate cast applied border, consisting of a molded inner section and outer edge of interlocking *C*-scrolls and shell motifs, is typical of English designs that were introduced by Huguenot makers by the early 1740s. Well-to-do American consumers certainly owned English silver, often ordered through agents abroad, where colonists might have a balance of credit due on goods (like crops) that were shipped to England. Although only rarely does an American history of ownership in the eighteenth century accompany a piece of English silver today, ownership records indicate that Peyton Randolph (c. 1721–1775) of Williamsburg, Virginia (a prominent patriot who served as president of the First Continental Congress), owned a pair of very similar London-made salvers.[38]

The visual connection between the Edwards salver and Winterthur's round tea table (fig. 21), as it would have been called in the eighteenth century, is obvious. Although this elaborately carved Philadelphia tea table was fashioned after English prototypes, the inspiration for this form—both abroad and in America—originally derived from the scalloped salver shape. In exceedingly wealthy, aristocratic families, oversized salvers with shaped surrounds might have been carried by a servant and placed upon a tea table with a top that echoed the shape of the silver salver, or waiter.[39] The top of this tea table is fashioned from a single plank of figured mahogany, with a molded edge carved from the solid piece in a sequence of reverse curves ornamented by eight carved flowerettes, one between each repeat. The top not only tilts to a vertical position for placement in a corner of a room or along a wall, but an open "box" (today referred to as a birdcage) fashioned with four turned pillars and attached to the top also allows it to turn on the columnar shaft, or pillar, of the base. In period references, this table would

**21** | Tea table, Philadelphia, 1765–1780 | The curvilinear design of the top of this tea table apparently derives from a similar form used for silver salvers (see fig. 20). Based on related English examples, round tilt-top tea tables such as this one became popular in America, especially in Philadelphia, during the third quarter of the eighteenth century.

have been called a pillar and claw table, and price books (guides for prices paid to journeymen) would have specified it as having a "Scollop'd Top & Carv'd Pillar"; a client would have paid extra for "Fluting the pillar" and for "Leaves on the knees."[40]

Some of the owners of such beautiful pieces took care to protect their investment at the time of the Revolution. Fearing that something untoward might happen in Philadelphia, Cadwalader (who left to command a battalion) asked his friend Jasper Yates of Lancaster, Pennsylvania, to protect the most valued furnishings. Yates, then in Philadelphia, wrote to his wife in Lancaster, reporting "Col. John Cadwalader has requested leave of me to store a part of his most valuable Furniture in our House. If it should come up to you in my Absence, you will please to have it put up in the Garret & have the Room locked up."[41] But only after the war actually escalated were cities evacuated, valuables stored away, and the social life of the elite interrupted.

Although the 1770s were tumultuous years, the colonists continued their lives with little recognition of the impending conflict. Houses were built, furniture was commissioned, portraits were painted. Looking at Charles Willson Peale's expressively serene portrait of the recently wed Julia Stockton Rush (fig. 22), viewers would never suspect what was occurring at about the time it was being painted. It was late June, into July of 1776: the Continental Congress was meeting in Philadelphia, and the Declaration of Independence was being written, read, and circulated amongst the colonists. Both Julia's husband, Dr. Benjamin Rush, and her father, Richard Stockton, were members of the Continental Congress and signers of the Declaration of Independence. Before the end of the year, Julia would see her husband, as well as Peale, go off to join Gen. John Cadwalader's battalion, which fought at Trenton and Princeton. Yet no hint of such a terrifying prospect appears in her painted countenance. On the contrary, playing on her elegant English guitar, she appears even more relaxed and at ease with the world than does Elizabeth Lloyd (fig. 15), whom Peale had painted five years earlier in a similar pose. Almost enveloped in rich drapery, Julia has the composure of an intelligent and sensible woman, which is further suggested by the books on the table beside her. The daughter of a lawyer and trustee of the College of New Jersey (Princeton), she grew up in a home where her father's library was reputed to be among the best in the colonies.

When Julia Stockton married Dr. Benjamin Rush in January 1776, she was fourteen years his junior. He had already gained a reputation as a contentious, outspoken, and often inflammatory critic of contemporary colonial politics. He was distrustful of the rule of the assembly, what he referred to as "mobocracy," and though he participated in the Revolution (serving as a doctor to Cadwalader's battalion of the Pennsylvania

militia), by 1779 he wrote to Charles Lee, stating "my family and my business now engross all my time and attention. My country I have long ago left to the care of Timy. Matlack, Tom Paine, Charles Willson Peale, & Co."[42] In 1783–1786, when Peale commenced and completed this companion portrait of Rush (fig. 23), the heat of heightened political feelings had cooled and Rush presumably chose to be portrayed (and remembered) as a sensitive, studious member of the intellectual and humanistic post-Revolutionary Philadelphia Society.[43] Casually seated in his study, garbed in an informal lounging coat, or banyan, Rush appears as the scholar and philosopher that he was. Rush himself commented in his medical lectures that "Loose dresses contribute to the ease and vigorous exercise of the faculties of the mind....we find that studious men are always painted in gowns, when they are seated in their libraries."[44]

In New York, a city that certainly attracted several talented rococo artisans, the furniture produced between 1750 and 1785 differed significantly from that fashioned by Philadelphians during the same period. For example, the Philadelphia side chair (fig. 24, left), is in its overall form and embellishment dramatically different from the New York chair (fig. 24, right). Each is indicative of the city in which it was made: the Philadelphia example is more elaborate, more rococo, with the pierced splat comprising a series of interlocking *C*-scrolls and the crest-rail across the top having very pronounced, boldly carved ears. The New York example has limited foliate carving, and the rear stiles are molded, whereas those on the Philadelphia side chair are fully carved with delicate trailing foliage, flowers, and fruits, a highly rococo embellishment. Much of the carving

on the splat of the New York example is in the manner of ruffles, or simple gadrooned decoration. Although the cabriole legs on both chairs have fully carved knees, the style of carving on the Philadelphia example is more sculptural, flowing, and naturalistic than the very stylized, linear leafage on the knees of the New York chair. Why are these chairs so different? Economics was not necessarily a factor, for both chairs were commissioned by well-to-do, important families.[45] Presumably, client choice and craftsman's background and ability determined these dramatically different interpretations.

Just as Charles Willson Peale had traveled south to Maryland to fulfill some commissions, in June 1771 the now mature John Singleton Copley left Boston to paint the elite of New York. During a six-month stay, he and his wife were feted and entertained as if they were dignitaries, so pleased the New York elite must have been to have an accomplished artist of (by now) significant reputation to take their likenesses. Copley's captivating portrait of Mary Philipse Morris (fig. 25) epitomizes his finest work from this period. Strikingly simple and serene, the forty-year-old wife of Roger Morris appears as a woman of breeding, stature, and intelligence. In obvious contrast to Peale's portrayals of equally affluent women, Copley depicted Mary Morris without voluminous, rich costume and drapery. Personality prevails, not pomp. A striking similarity exists between Copley's depiction of Mary Morris and that of her close friend Margaret Gage (Mrs. Thomas).[46] Both women married British officers and led parallel lives. Born into one of New York's most notable old Dutch families, Mary grew up at Philipse Manor on the Hudson River, long the seat of her ancestors. An intelligent beauty as well as a young woman of substantial means, Mary was pursued by numerous young men. Instead of an American, she chose an English officer, Roger Morris, who had served in the Hudson Valley campaigns during the French and Indian Wars. By the mid-1760s they had built a grand mansion on Harlem Heights, with great vistas of Long Island and New York. Though much altered since the Morrises lived there, this house today stands as the Morris-Jumel Mansion at West 160th Street and Edgecombe Avenue. Though the Morrises had hoped to stay in New York, by 1783 their lands had been confiscated by the state and they sailed for England, never to return. Copley's portrait went with them, as Morris had instructed his wife, saying "Copley's Performance I beg may be particularly taken care of."[47]

Although in size the fourth largest colonial city, Charleston, South Carolina, might be thought of as the "London of the South" in the decades leading up to and immediately following the Revolution: it exceeded all others in average wealth per capita and quite probably in the taste and sophistication of its elite. Largely owing to Charleston's longstanding export trade with England, primarily in rice and indigo, South Caro-

**25** | *Mrs. Roger Morris,* John Singleton Copley, New York, 1771 | Mary Philipse married English officer Roger Morris, who had served in the French and Indian Wars. Since her husband would not fight in the Revolutionary War, the couple moved to England for two years, returned to America, and then later (with their two daughters) permanently relocated to England, where Mary died at the age of ninety-six.

26 | *John Purves and His Wife Eliza Anne Pritchard*, Henry Benbridge, Charleston, South Carolina, 1775–1777 | Fashion-conscious Charlestonians such as John Purves and his wife Eliza Anne wished to emulate English society through portraits and other furnishings. Artist Henry Benbridge, lately returned from England, was ready and willing to oblige, deriving the pose of the Purveses from conventional English paintings or printed sources that he saw when studying in London.

linians looked to London as their center of fashion and culture more than to their northern neighbors. Because of the excessive affluence gained from these agricultural pursuits, wealthy Charlestonians had the means of furnishing their homes with London-made goods ranging from expensive furniture to smaller items such as silver and rich cut glass. As Bostonian Josiah Quincy Jr. observed of Charleston in 1773, "in grandeur, splendour of buildings, decorations, equipages, numbers, commerce, shipping, indeed in almost every thing, it far surpasses all I ever saw or expected to see in America."[48] Reflecting upon earlier days in Charleston, John Drayton wrote in 1802, "Charlestonians sought in every possible way to emulate the life of London society. They were too much enamoured of British customs, manners and education to imagine that elsewhere anything of advantage could be obtained."[49] When artist Henry Benbridge (1743–1812) arrived in Charleston, he was well prepared to assist the local elite in emulating the English at least in the manner and style of the portraiture they commissioned. In 1764 Benbridge (who had been born into a Philadelphia family of some means) was able to go to London and Italy to study painting when he reached his majority (and received his inheritance). Benbridge returned to the colonies in 1769, and by 1772 had traveled to Charleston to settle into the role of image-maker. With his knowledge of European portraiture (he had studied in the studio of Pompeo Batoni in Italy) and English aristocratic style, he was able to meet the demands of a wealthy planter clientele who perhaps wished to be more English than the English.

Benbridge's double portrait of the recently married Capt. and Mrs. John Purves (fig. 26), painted 1775–1777, is every bit as urbane and sophisticated as the images Peale painted of the Lloyds, Cadwaladers, and Rushes, and the picture Copley painted of Mary Morris, though Benbridge did not have quite the talent of his contemporaries. Much of Benbridge's work reveals the influence of his mentors, especially that of his fellow Pennsylvanian expatriate, Benjamin West, by whom he was greatly influenced during his tenure in London. While many portraits of the period reinforce the increasingly compassionate nature of marriages in the late eighteenth century, few sitters are portrayed as equally as the Purveses are. They occupy the same portion of the picture plane and are given comparable space. Anne Purves reinforces their closeness by leaning on her husband.

**27** | Slab-top side table, possibly South Carolina or Philadelphia, 1760–1775; Sweetmeat pole and baskets, England, 1760–1780; Salver, England, 1760–1785; Jelly glasses, England, 1760–1785 | Surrounded by jelly glasses atop a glass salver, this towering sweetmeat pole would have made a dramatic visual impact when the glasses and hanging baskets were filled with sparkling, colorful jellies and candied fruits and nuts.

Although Charlestonians imported quantities of elegant English furniture for their substantial homes, quite competent local cabinetmakers were also able to meet the challenge of competing with goods from abroad. A mahogany frame with marble slab (fig. 27) is a rare example of what may have been a relatively popular form in the second half of the eighteenth century. Essentially the forerunner of the more numerous, new fashion sideboards of the Federal period, this side table would have probably been used in a dining room, where the marble top would have been resistant to the heat and wetness of various dishes and liquid refreshments. The subtle shaping across the front of the skirt, combined with the bold rococo carving on the cabriole legs, makes this side table one of the most refined to have survived. Although Joe Kindig Jr. sold this table to du Pont in 1939 as a "Philadelphia marbletop Chippendale Table of unusually fine quality, c. 1770.... $10,000," a decade later du Pont's curator Joseph Downs learned that it had been purchased in Columbia, South Carolina, by Harry Aarons and Kindig. In 1970 even more of its history was revealed; it had been bought about the turn of the century in Columbia from a local antique dealer, a Mr. Weinsel, who "had purchased it himself in lower South Carolina."[50] Although it is tempting to attribute this table frame to a Charleston, South Carolina, shop, at this time evidence of a specific place of origin is not conclusive. While the yellow pine secondary wood could suggest a southern origin, it could also place the manufacture of this table in the mid-Atlantic region.

A uniquely American manifestation of the rococo can be seen in the famed Rhode Island block-and-shell pieces (fig. 28), which are among the most highly admired and desired case furniture from New England in this period. The precise inspiration, the source, for this distinctive and singularly impressive form does not seem to lie in English or European designs. While the blockfront form does have some precedent abroad, and was undoubtedly first produced in Boston probably by the early to mid-1730s, the Rhode Island rendition, which incorporates convex and concave shells surmounting the blocking, may actually be one of the few distinctly American innovations. In addition to the high caliber of carving seen in the shells, the selection of an extraordinary quality of mahogany, and the superior "engineering" and construction of these pieces, their overall presence has captivated both original owners and collectors for over two centuries.

How much of the rococo taste do these Rhode Island pieces embody? Although they are quite linear and in a sense austere, the carved shell certainly captures the *rocaille* sense, echoing in a very ordered way the aspect of a shell-encrusted grotto. What inspired the cabinetmakers of Rhode Island to create this imaginative and highly labor-intensive type of ornament? Emanating from Newport, a port town on the southernmost tip of the island of Aquidneck, this idea, it is tempting to think, may have had

something to do with the omnipresence of the sea and its bounty. Two Quaker cabinet-making families, the Goddards and the Townsends, with roots on the northern shore of Long Island, were the principal progenitors of this block-and-shell furniture. However, recent scholarship has revealed that a small group of block-and-shell pieces of furniture was also produced in Providence, Rhode Island, a city that did not suffer the economic devastation experienced by Newport during the Revolution.[51] On the contrary, enterprising merchants in Providence, such as the Brown brothers, profited from the war, and when peace came they continued their lifestyle in an even more affluent manner. The great nine-shell chest-on-chest (fig. 28) is one of these Providence-made block-and-shell examples; it is also one of only two known pieces having nine shells (the other is a desk and bookcase also made in Providence). Both nine-shell pieces were commissioned by Browns: the desk and bookcase by Joseph and Winterthur's chest-on-chest either by Joseph or his daughter Eliza Brown Ward. Made of highly figured, carefully selected mahogany, the Providence group of block-and-shell furniture can be identified from the Newport group by several different design and construction features. Perhaps most distinctive among these is the shells, which are not carved then applied, but rather carved from the solid plank of mahogany. The result of this method, which was actually more labor intensive and risky, is that the shells are bolder and bounded with a scribed circumference, the inner edge of which is carved out below the plane of the drawer front.

Henry Francis du Pont's intense interest in the rococo style, in its "widely differing products of regions showing different influences—Boston, Newport, New York, Philadelphia [and Charleston]," vividly reflects his eclectic taste. Thanks to this inveterate collector's keen persistence and pursuit of the most interesting, the unusual, and the finest, Winterthur can today provide the novice, the student, and the advanced collector with a broad and illuminating experience of the rococo taste in America.

**28** | Chest-on-chest, Providence, Rhode Island, 1775–1790; Carved shell (detail of chest) | While not based precisely on European rococo prototypes, the innovative design of Rhode Island block-and-shell furniture reinterpreted elements relating to the rococo, such as the carved shells and the undulating movement of the chest's façade. Its distinctively bold shells were carved from a solid piece of mahogany, hence distinguishing this Providence-made piece from its Newport relations (whose shells were carved and then applied to the drawer front).

# 4. The Arts of the Pennsylvania Germans

THE GERMANIC PEOPLE WHO TRAVELED to America in the eighteenth century, like most other immigrants, came primarily for opportunity and economic freedom. As they interfaced with the inhabitants, who were primarily English, their language, values, customs, and habits were subjected to compromise and acculturation. Some native-born Anglo-Americans were apprehensive of the new arrivals. In 1751 Benjamin Franklin referred to them as *Palatine Boors* and feared that Pennsylvania would soon become a "colony of *Aliens*" where these transplanted peoples would "shortly be so numerous as to Germanize us instead of our Anglifying them." Although Franklin's apprehensions were unfulfilled,[1] they were not unfounded in some respects: by the time of the first United States census in 1790, German-Swiss settlers made up one-third of the population in Pennsylvania, and nearly forty percent in the southeastern region of the state.[2] Yet as these diverse cultures interacted, each absorbed elements of the other for a variety of reasons, be they economic, practical, or simply preferential. Thus today survives a large body of distinctly "American" material possessions made by these Germanic settlers that reveals much about the surroundings they valued most in their daily lives.

Skilled artisans, tradesmen, farmers, and religious leaders were among those Germanic settlers who came to the New World from a variety of areas in the Holy Roman Empire. The majority of those who inhabited Pennsylvania lived in nonurban, agrarian areas and small rural towns. Germantown (a part of Philadelphia) was the urban locus of their culture, and the county seats of Lancaster, York, and Reading eventually became smaller urban centers of commercial, intellectual, and religious congregation. These Germanic settlers practiced a variety of religions. While almost 90 percent were Lutherans and German Reformed Church members, the remaining 10 percent included Mennonites, Moravians, Schwenkfelders, Presbyterians, and Roman Catholics. Yet superseding this religious diversity were common cultural bonds that united them. They were an industrious people, hardworking and religious. Many, especially those engaged in intellectual or commercial pursuits, were bilingual. In 1789 Benjamin Rush began *An Account of the Manners of the German Inhabitants of Pennsylvania* by proclaiming that "The *State of Pennsylvania* is so much indebted for her prosperity and reputation to the *German* part of her citizens."[3]

Early in the twentieth century enterprising dealers and collectors "discovered" the aesthetic beauty and accomplishments represented in many of the objects these Germanic settlers produced. Although Henry Francis du Pont was first smitten by historic New England objects, almost immediately upon returning to the Delaware Valley from a trip north in 1923, he began to acquire objects produced centuries before in his own "backyard," Pennsylvania.[4] Other astute early collectors who were also stricken by the mania for collecting Pennsylvania German objects included Titus Geesey (also from Delaware) and J. Stodgell Stokes. Many of the items acquired by these latter collectors are now in the collections of the Philadelphia Museum of Art.

If there was one common perspective that these Germanic immigrants brought from central Europe, it was the desire, perhaps even need (instilled as a cultural construct), to embellish their everyday lives with color, ornament, and celebration. Of course, not everything they owned and used on a daily basis was ornamented, but important events —births, baptisms, betrothals, marriages, or even just educational accomplishments— were often celebrated with special gifts. These tokens were frequently embellished with the recipient's initials, name(s), date, and various, sometimes symbolic, ornamental motifs. Painted chests, small decorated boxes (fig. 1), and fraktur (a term derived from

**1** | Box, Berks or Northampton County, Pennsylvania, 1770–1800 | This diminutive box, or miniature chest, illustrates the skill of the Pennsylvania German decorative painter in its orderly and precise design motifs. A compass was used to define the trefoil design, and scribe lines are still visible on the front of the box.

**2** | Chest, Berks County, Pennsylvania, 1765–1810 | Chests often held important objects, such as bibles and family documents, as well as personal items like clothing and bedding. Not all chests were as elaborately decorated as this one, but those that were probably marked significant events.

a German word meaning "to write fancily") are what today qualifies as quintessentially Pennsylvania German or Dutch (a misnomer for Deutsch). Though these useful, highly decorated objects are a part of the material heritage handed down by this distinct cultural group for enlightenment and enjoyment, they represent only one aspect of the creative impulse with which these settlers filled their lives.

Chests, or chists as they often are called in period documents, were perhaps the most essential piece of household furniture of the eighteenth and nineteenth centuries. They provide an excellent example of acculturation, for the form is English (Anglo) and the construction and decoration is Germanic. They were made in numerous configurations, with and without drawers, and in various woods—some, like white-and-yellow pine and tulip wood, were always painted; others, such as walnut, were occasionally embellished with inlay. All manner of painted ornament can be found on these chests, and some façades were even faced with additional wood to create a more architectural presentation. For today's collectors, the most desirable painted chests are those with elaborate ornamental motifs, names, and dates. However, such pieces represent the minority of those made; many chests did not mark a specific occasion and were simply painted one color, with perhaps the base molding and feet painted black. Sometimes these chests were painted in two colors: a base coat embellished with various sponged or squiggle motifs referred to in the period as speckled. The urge to elaborate even upon the most basic must have been omnipresent in the hands of many artisans as well as in the minds of those who commissioned this work.

Although today many people refer to these painted chests as dower chests (part of and for the storage of a young woman's marriage dowry), it should be noted that men also owned chests. While women's names appear on many chests with visual documentation (names and dates), an almost equal number of chests survive bearing men's names. For example, a unicorn chest related in decoration to a chest at Winterthur (fig. 2) is inscribed with the name Heinrich Faust (1766–1825) and dated 1784.[5] Faust, a second generation native Pennsylvania German, was born in Bern Township, Berks County, a region noted for the production of a group of chests decorated with unicorns, men brandishing swords astride galloping horses, and distinctive sawtooth borders framing the arched panels on the façades. Though many chests have lost their original histories, those pieces with names and dates have provided helpful clues in determining the specific areas where they were fashioned; hence, the varied motifs and patterns of ornamentation have been regionalized. Because painted chests are only occasionally signed by their makers or decorators, attributions are primarily limited to specific counties in Pennsylvania; sometimes more specific attributions can be made to townships.

Who were the painters who ornamented these chests and other small wooden items, and where did they get their ideas for such seemingly fanciful motifs? Since the number of firmly documented pieces is limited, no more than a handful of makers have been identified.[6] Sometimes these joiners, carpenters, or cabinetmakers were themselves the painters decorating these chests, as is evidenced today in surviving chests signed by Christian Seltzer. But chests were also very likely ornamented (or at least influenced) by a second artisan, perhaps a multitalented painter of signs, carriages, or fraktur. In Milford Township, Bucks County, John Drissell (active 1790–1817), the son of a carpenter, was responsible for the ornament on a number of small items including salt boxes, tape looms, and even a spoon cabinet.[7] Drissell's ornament and letters resemble the work of a Lutheran schoolmaster and fraktur artist, John Adam Eÿer, who taught at schools attended by the young women for whom Drissell made these items. Presumably Drissell was influenced by Eÿer's artful work, or maybe he took instruction from this talented artist.

While much of this ornament evidences creative talents, the forms and motifs themselves were sometimes age-old, such as the image of Adam and Eve seen on one chest (see fig. 12). Many of these images were gleaned from printed sources, such as illustrations in Bibles, imported engravings, local broadsides, and even printed textiles.[8] For instance, the unicorn motif may have been derived from any number of images of the British coat of arms—an interpretation positing an interesting melding of English imagery with Germanic forms and decoration. Some have even assigned a religious

**3** | Fraktur, possibly Mahantango Valley, Pennsylvania, about 1798 | The fanciful decoration on this *Taufschein* (birth certificate) surrounds the factual information about Johannes Kreniger's 1798 birth and baptism with symbols of his culture.

meaning to the imagery of the unicorn. Such a universal motif, however, undoubtedly embraced layers of symbolism depending on the perception and perspective of the maker, patron, and viewer. However, one fact remains indisputable: these highly embellished objects celebrated occasions, marking a coming of age or, for many, a new embarkation in life.

Those objects most symbolic of the stages of life were the colorful fraktur that marked births, baptisms, marriages, and even deaths that were documented in a family record. Small fanciful drawings were also presented to students as rewards of merit for scholarly accomplishments; often undocumented in any way, these works too held important personal significance. Sometimes these paper records were affixed inside the lids of chests or boxes as a way of keeping them safe from harm and close to their owner's private possessions. A fraktur attached inside the lid of a chest at Winterthur (fig. 2) depicts Adam and Eve in the Garden of Eden; although it is not a marriage certificate, the accompanying verses of the story of Adam and Eve suggest that a marriage was proposed and that this chest must have been presented upon a betrothal.

Another fraktur (fig. 3) echoes some of the same motifs seen on the chest (fig. 2), including the pair of rampant unicorns, the arched-head tablet, and the proverbial tulips and birds. Drawn by an unidentified artist, presumably working in the Mahantango

Valley region of Northumberland County, this *Taufschein* (birth certificate) documents the safe arrival of Johannes Kreniger, born to Heinrich and Anna Maria Kreniger on 26 June 1798. It also records that Pastor Moeller baptized him, and Wilhelm and Barbara Keim sponsored him. The marvelous smiling lions above the unicorns recall the British arms, suggesting that the artist has imaginatively copied his motifs from a more academic source, reconfiguring the animal forms in this wholly symmetrical format. The winged angel face in the lunette atop the tablet recalls tombstones, but may also be symbolic of angelic blessings on the newborn. The paired birds across the bottom and flanking the vase with central tulip and trailing vines are motifs common to many fraktur, but the manner in which they are rendered and the distinctive salmon, brown, and mustard coloration of this piece are unusual. This particular fraktur artist may have seen a Berks County unicorn chest brought westward to Northumberland County and may have adapted, in his own inspired way, some of the motifs for this brilliantly conceived *Taufschein*.

Not all immigrants of Germanic heritage settled in eastern Pennsylvania; some went directly to areas in Virginia and North Carolina, while others later migrated southward from Pennsylvania into the Valley of Virginia and beyond. Similar traditions, however, were embraced by these southern Germans, as a fascinating fraktur (fig. 4) attests. Penned by fraktur artist, school teacher, and Mennonite minister Jacob Strickler (1770–1842), this *Zierschrift* (decorative writing) presents a totally asymmetrical composition that is dramatically different from the strict symmetrical format of many other fraktur, including the Kreniger *Taufschein* (fig. 3). Strickler was descended from Swiss Mennonites who had settled first in Lancaster County, Pennsylvania, and by 1733 had moved south to an area of Shenandoah County called Massanutten.[9] A talented and highly creative artist, Strickler was related by marriage to the furniture decorator Johannes Spitler, who imaginatively painted chests and clock cases that definitely suggest some influence or collaboration with Strickler.[10]

The Valley of Virginia and the North Carolina Moravian settlements at Bethabara and Salem fostered numerous other talented artists and artisans working in all media, though the early potters are especially noteworthy.[11] The bulk of their production, like the work of most artisans, focused on utilitarian wares, but their ornamented, slip-decorated pieces—sometimes with designs following northern European prototypes—allowed for greater aesthetic expression. Perhaps in imitation of imported ornamental figures, wholly nonutilitarian objects were occasionally produced. Although probably made in Waynesboro, Pennsylvania, John Bell Sr.'s whimsical, toothy lion (fig. 5) is similar to other lions made by Bell family members working in the Shenandoah Valley

of Virginia. The son of Peter Bell Jr., a potter in Elizabeth Town (now Hagerstown), Maryland, John Bell Sr. first worked in his father's pottery. In 1824 Peter moved his family to Winchester, Virginia, where he established a pottery, working with his sons John, Samuel, and Solomon. In 1827, the year following his marriage, John relocated to Chambersburg, Pennsylvania, and by 1833 opened a pottery in Waynesboro.

In almost every media produced, earlier traditions survived well into the nineteenth century in backcountry areas. Painted furniture, sometimes elaborately decorated, continued to be produced because, first and foremost, it was made from plentiful, inexpensive, locally harvested woods such as white-and-yellow pine and tulip. A particularly fascinating and distinctive group of case furniture was produced in the second quarter of the nineteenth century in an isolated, rural area of Northumberland County, just east of the Susquehanna River. Often referred to as Mahantango Valley furniture, these pieces were, we now believe, very likely made in the nearby region of the Schwaben Creek Valley.[12] Solidly constructed of white pine and tulip, these pieces are often painted with a combination of two shades of green (one of which tends toward very blue-green). As illustrated by the Masser desk (fig. 6), this colorful furniture is decorated with red, yellow, and black motifs of birds, horses, trees, and compass stars in a well-ordered and engaging manner. Although at first these designs might appear quite unique and individual, closer study reveals that they were probably derived from a variety of printed fraktur produced from the early nineteenth century onward. Thus, these designs represent yet another example of inspired copy work by rural decorators.[13] Painted in small lettering across the front of this desk is "JACOB 1834 MASER," the name of the original owner. Born in 1812, Masser was a farmer and a carpenter. He was twenty-two years old when he acquired this desk in 1834, the year that he married Catharine Christ. As a case of drawers for the storage of clothing and linens, as well as a desk, this piece was perhaps the equivalent of a dower chest for Jacob Masser. Interestingly, Jacob Masser's desk was among Henry Francis du Pont's earliest purchases of painted Pennsylvania German furniture. He acquired it in 1929, along with a related chest of drawers, from the Bethlehem dealer, A.H. Rice, who had advertised it (and ten other pieces) in *The Magazine Antiques* in December 1926 as "collected by me in Remote areas of Pennsylvania." Rice asked $700 for both the desk and chest "delivered to Winterthur." So taken was du Pont with this group of green decorated furniture that by the time he opened Winterthur as a museum in 1951 he owned five Schwaben Creek Valley pieces.

The exuberance, richness, and ornament of Pennsylvania German production was not restricted to painted furniture and fraktur. Readily available native hardwoods such as black walnut, cherry, and maple were chosen when the client had the resources or aesthetic inclination to order a more expensive and stylish object. Perhaps the most Germanic as well as monumental form was the *Kleiderschrank*, or *Glederschang* (clothes cupboard), which was made in a variety of woods, some hard and unpainted, some soft and thus painted. This type of object, like the dower chest, would have been acquired by a young couple to mark a marriage and the beginning of a new life. Since eighteenth-century German houses rarely had closets, a clothes and linen cupboard was an essential piece of furniture for a young couple to acquire as they set up housekeeping. A magnificent Lancaster County *Schrank* (fig. 7) was presumably made for the marriage of Emanuel and Mary Herr, whose names and marriage date (1768) are inscribed with sulfur inlay in the upper panels of the doors. Clearly the symbolism of the ornamental inlay suggests marriage, with a large bird atop the inlaid foliate cartouche of the upper left panel (inscribed with Emanuel's name) and two smaller birds (though one is larger than the other) touching beaks atop the cartouche with Mary Herr's name in it. The entwined serpentines in the lower panels symbolize love's true knot: the everlasting union of two persons. An overall baroque design aesthetic pervades this boldly executed

6 | Desk, Schwaben Creek Valley, Pennsylvania, 1834 | During the second quarter of the nineteenth century, a distinctively decorated group of painted case furniture was produced in a very rural area known as the Schwaben Creek Valley. The motifs ornamenting this desk exemplify the simple yet whimsical decoration that graces many of these pieces.

**7** | *Schrank*, Lancaster County, Pennsylvania, 1768 | An essential piece of furniture, for most eighteenth-century dwellings had few closets, this *Kleiderschrank* (clothespress) was presumably acquired by Emanuel and Mary Herr about the time of their marriage in 1768.

*Schrank* in the inlaid patterns, the unusual relief carving flanking the drawers in the base, the original flattened ball feet, and the bold ogee moldings of the base and cornice.

Proportionately monumental and even more baroque in design than the *Schrank* are the four pewter candlesticks (fig. 8) made by the Moravian emigré pewterer Johann Christoph Heyne (1715–1781). Born in Saxony, Heyne learned his trade in Germany and worked as a journeyman in Stockholm prior to arriving in Philadelphia in 1742 with other members of the Unitas Fratrum (Moravian Church). He first settled and worked in Bethlehem, Pennsylvania (the political seat of the Moravian Church), but later moved to Berks County, and by 1757 had finally settled in Lancaster, where he worked until his death in 1781. As evidenced by these elaborately conceived ecclesiastical candlesticks, Heyne was well versed in the late seventeenth-century baroque style that had surrounded him in the land of his youth. These masterfully executed candlesticks echo those found in churches across central Europe in the late seventeenth and early eighteenth centuries. Embellished with Jesuit symbolism showing the six symbols of Christ's passion, these four candlesticks are presumably part of a set of six made for the altar of the Most Blessed Sacrament (Catholic) Church in Bally, Berks County. That this deeply religious Moravian artisan made these impressive icons of Catholicism for one of the few religious minorities in the predominantly Protestant Delaware Valley is fascinating.

While some traditional European and Germanic forms were singularly copied in America (as were the Heyne candlesticks), other forms were more universally embraced and became a regional standard. One example of this phenomenon is evidenced in the popular preference for the turned post, slat-back chair throughout the Delaware Valley region in New Jersey, eastern Pennsylvania, and Delaware. A traditional, affordable piece of seating furniture produced over several centuries in the low countries and central Europe, this form was made with a myriad of variations ranging from choice of woods, number of slats, elaboration of turning, and surface finish. Winterthur's slat-back side chairs (fig. 9) represent this traditional form carried to the height of its aesthetic achievement. The chair on the left, made of maple with a nicely figured striped maple used for the turned posts, shows an especially fine gradation of the tapering of the five slats as they increase in depth from the lowermost to the uppermost slat. Also above the norm are the shaped facings applied to the sides of the seat rails, the boldly turned front stretcher, and the elaborate turnings of the front legs ending in flattened ring turnings at the bottom. This product, the result of consumer choice and economic conservatism, represents a keen eye for design on the part of the craftsman. The less usual slat-back chair on the right is a lively variation on the theme; although not as brilliantly conceived, it is an interesting translation of a distinct regional interpretation.

**8** | Candlesticks (two of a set of four), Johann Christoph Heyne, Lancaster, Pennsylvania, 1752–1781 | These monumental ecclesiastical pewter candlesticks were fashioned in a fully realized baroque style, strongly reflecting objects Heyne was familiar with from his training as a youth in Germany.

**9** | Slat-back side chair, Delaware Valley, Pennsylvania, 1725–1750; Slat-back side chair, Delaware Valley, Pennsylvania, 1725–1750 | Two variations on a popular theme, these chairs reflect both consumer choice and craftsman's creativity. A wide variety of slat-back chairs were popular throughout the Delaware Valley region in New Jersey, Pennsylvania, and Delaware.

**10** | Armchair, Bethlehem, Pennsylvania, 1770–1800; Armchair, Lancaster, Pennsylvania, 1753–1773 | Intriguing in both their design and execution, these leather-upholstered armchairs appear to be products of Moravian craftsmen who merged both English and European influences to create distinctively different versions of seating furniture.

Perhaps the useful arts of the Pennsylvania Germans are so appealing and intriguing because in many instances they result from the merging of Germanic and Anglo-American traditions. As traditional forms, decorative patterns, and methods of execution were transferred to America, the objects made in this country underwent a natural mutation as physical circumstance and influences from other cultures combined with the personal interpretation of the artisan or patron. Sometimes the result clung closely to tradition, as in the case of Heyne's candlesticks (fig. 8) and the two slat-back side chairs (fig. 9). In other instances, such as Winterthur's two leather-upholstered armchairs (fig. 10), a new breed, so to speak, was born. Presumably made by Moravian craftsmen (the one on the left probably in the Moravian settlement of Bethlehem, the one on the right perhaps closer to Lancaster), these chairs reflect a certain Anglo-influence on a characteristic central European theme. Although related Germanic precedents can be cited for both leather armchairs, details such as the shaped crest with its central carved shell and distinctive ears, and the cabriole legs with unusual pointed feet represent both Anglo-influence and individual interpretation. Similarly, the armchair on the left is a combination of Germanic tradition, Anglo-influence, and individual innovation—as seen in the flat baluster-shaped arm supports.

Henry Francis du Pont desired to place his Pennsylvania German arts in appropriate architectural contexts, just as he had installed his more formal, urban furniture and related objects in rooms such as the Port Royal Parlor (chapter 3, fig. 16) and the Stamper-Blackwell Parlor (chapter 3, fig. 1). In 1950 he was finally able to acquire an extraordinary painted architectural interior from the David Hottenstein (1734–1802) house, a major stone domicile just north of Kutztown in Berks County[14] (fig. 11). Taken from the second floor, this space was called the Great Room in Hottenstein's 1802 inventory. Du Pont dubbed it the Fraktur Room (fig. 12) for the large number of colorful celebratory certificates from his collection that soon graced the walls. Its notable painted and grained woodwork blended nicely with the fraktur and the painted and decorated pieces of furniture that du Pont placed there. In the center of the room, he installed a great long walnut table with a typically Germanic $X$-form base (today called a sawbuck table by collectors). By 1958 he had been able to acquire Hottenstein's enormous walnut clothespress, with the inlaid date of 1781 (probably the year Hottenstein married his wife Catherine). A significant Germanic baroque form with German construction features, this piece had been purchased by an Easton, Pennsylvania, collector, Asher Odenwelder Jr., in 1950 at the time that the interior woodwork was removed from the house for du Pont.

**13** | Fraktur Room mantel, with milk pan, John Strawn, Bucks County, Pennsylvania, 1797 | The painted decoration on the paneling from the Hottenstein House is among the most remarkable and best preserved of its date in eastern Pennsylvania. The sgraffito milk pan has a humorous verse inscribed around the rim: "Py and Cream Was thare Sceem this Thing its Past amongs the youth thay Can not Deny & Speak the truth / This thing it Caused them to Comply Witch they Cannot Deny you have it as Cheap as I March 10th 1797 John Strawn."

Although the painted decoration on the fireplace paneling and the woodwork in this room might be perceived as part of a centuries-old European tradition of painted simulation, it probably derived more directly from a similar preference found in south German baroque interiors, especially church architecture. The asymmetrical design of the paneling on the fireplace wall is particularly unusual and does not follow traditional English precedents. The painted decoration of this paneling (fig. 13) is among the most remarkable and best preserved of its date in the eastern Pennsylvania region. Worked into the mottled paint of the two vertical panels are great floral motifs, and similarly large multipetaled blossoms ornament the panels in the doors of this room. Though worn with time and age, this paneling continues to project its original intent: announcing a richness and elaboration presumably well above that of any other house of its period in this once rural Berks County region. A second generation German, Hottenstein chose to build a typical English Georgian house to proclaim his status: as the prime taxpayer in Maxatawney Township, he was presumably the wealthiest inhabitant (Hottenstein was a farmer who also owned a still, and it is difficult to say which resource provided his great wealth). Although Hottenstein's house in general character follows English architectural traditions, many of its details speak with a German accent, presumably because of the involvement of local German tradesmen in its building and decoration. For example, the iron door hinges and locks are Germanic, as is the use of stoves in front of fireplaces.

In a manner similar to that seen in the Hottenstein house, a desk and bookcase (fig. 14) is in form essentially English classical with a Germanic accent. The overall design and execution of this piece present a combination of sophistication and economy. Made of white pine, this desk and bookcase was, from the initial concept, intended to be painted. The different colors and techniques, in addition to the actual design features, make it a most successful and appealing alternative to a more expensive piece, such as one made of native walnut. Echoing more urban examples, the engaged quarter columns, fluted pilasters, broken-scroll pediment, and applied carving on the tympanum of the upper case suggest that both patron and craftsman were familiar with high-style variations made in Philadelphia or possibly Lancaster. The technique of first applying an overall coat of white paint before selectively adding blue paint allowed the columns and pediment molding to remain white and thus frame the entire piece, as was occasionally done in hardwoods on urban examples. The tapering of the broken-scroll pediment molding is unusual and may help to determine where this piece was made. Instead of painting the panels of the doors, drawer front, and sides of the upper and lower cases to simulate the grain of a more expensive wood, the decorator (in an almost whimsical manner) has suggested great, flowing flowers—perhaps carnations—in these areas.

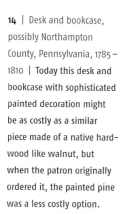

**14** | Desk and bookcase, possibly Northampton County, Pennsylvania, 1785–1810 | Today this desk and bookcase with sophisticated painted decoration might be as costly as a similar piece made of a native hardwood like walnut, but when the patron originally ordered it, the painted pine was a less costly option.

**15** | Interior of desk and bookcase (detail of fig. 14) | This interior, which resembles those in urban desk and bookcases, suggests that the maker or patron was familiar with more costly, hardwood pieces. The interior paint, whose exposure to light, air, dirt, and dust was limited, retains much of the original vivid color.

The interior of the desk (fig. 15) is as fully articulated as any found in urban examples; the paint retains much of its original vibrancy and color, with a salmon hue framing the vertical document drawers and outlining the smaller drawers. Purchased in 1937 from the noted Pennsylvania dealer Hattie Brunner of Reinholds, Pennsylvania, this piece may have been made in Northampton County. However, no other related, nonurban examples employing this type of ingenuity and creativity survive to assist in documenting its place of origin. Until more information and other related examples come to light, the maker and owner of this remarkable desk and bookcase will remain a mystery.[15]

In an effort to demonstrate capability and ingenuity, craftsmen working in regions distant from major urban areas often produced amazingly complex and finely executed objects. Today these pieces are often described as naïve, folk, and, sometimes, unsophisticated. However, within the context of the society in which they were conceived, many of these objects were viewed as works of great accomplishment. The sheer number of examples of particular forms that survive suggests that these folk artists and artisans met their own and their patrons' expectations. This must have certainly been true of the extraordinary tall clock case (fig. 16) made in 1815 by John Paul Jr. of Washington Township, Dauphin County, Pennsylvania. Standing over eight feet tall, the paneled, carved, inlaid, and turned case of this clock is a tour de force of incomparable design and execution. What were the motives, talents, and money behind this very special commission? Although information concerning the patron who commissioned it is limited, the clock might have been acquired to celebrate a marriage. Family tradition relates that Paul

**16** | Tall clock, John Paul Jr., Elizabethville, Dauphin County, Pennsylvania, 1815 | Everything about this clock case suggests that the maker, John Paul Jr., considered it his master-work: the choice of highly figured wood, its great stature, the inlaid ornament and inscriptions, and the profusion of symbolic eagles all mark it as a singular accomplishment unlike any other of the region or period.

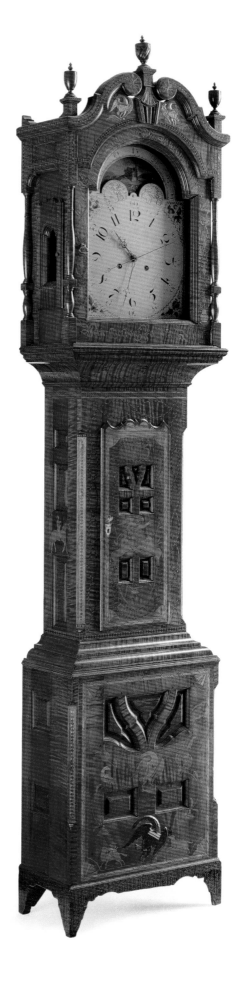

made this clock for Benjamin and Catherina Eva Graff Hammer, also of Washington Township, Dauphin County, and that the Hammers' possessions were a combination of some fine Philadelphia pieces and nonurban painted objects, like Benjamin's marriage chest (which was sold in the famous 1929 Howard Reifsnyder sale).[16] Interestingly, Catherina Eva was from a Philadelphia family with whom Thomas Jefferson had purportedly stayed during the Continental Congress. The unprecedented amount of inlaid script, naming the maker, place, and date completed, is better understood once more is revealed about John Paul Jr. Born in 1789 in Elizabethville, Dauphin County, Paul is remembered as a Renaissance man, for he was a brilliant engineer, architect, surveyor, cabinetmaker, and calligrapher.[17] Presumably, his first training was as a cabinetmaker, for this case was made when he was twenty-six years old. Later in his life he became involved in surveying and engineering, and in the early 1850s he designed a remarkable feat of railroad engineering, the famed Horseshoe Curve near Altoona, Pennsylvania.

**17** | Inlaid decoration (detail of fig. 16) | Paul's finely worked details — including the seal of the state of Pennsylvania, vines, tulips, and eagles — suggest that he challenged himself to master every skill in order to compete with both urban and nonurban craftsmen of the period.

Paul's creativity and passion for detail is proven in every aspect of this tall clock. The curled maple selected for the primary structure, the contrasting lighter woods of the inlaid and carved portions, and the carefully molded portions all echo his determination to craft something unlike anything ever before attempted. The carved and inlaid ornament that covers much of the entire façade evokes both patriotic as well as traditional Germanic symbolism. The seal of the state of Pennsylvania is inlaid on the door (fig. 17), flanked by vines and tulips, while nine images of eagles appear from the top of the broken-scroll pediment to the center of the base. Much of the inlaid and molded decoration can be traced to the design of German furniture of the late eighteenth century, raising the possibility that Paul was working from observation of actual objects that may have come to Dauphin County with emigré settlers. Although many unanswered questions still surround this exemplary commission, it is unquestionably a masterwork of backcountry artisanry.

Just as John Paul Jr. used eagle imagery as ornament on his clock case, a German emigré woodcarver named Wilhelm Schimmel (1817–1890) also focused, over half a century later, on eagles (fig. 18), crafting sculptural birds and other animals that he painted in strong colors. Schimmel's work is part of a long tradition of whittling and carving that occurred in rural areas of America over several centuries and recalled earlier European traditions. The distinctive nature of his eagle carvings was probably not unique to Schimmel, for they appear to derive from Germanic emblems that he could have been familiar with during his youth abroad.[18] Today collectors covet the products of numerous unknown artisans, admiring these objects for their (in our eyes) simplistic and often whimsical expressions. But how were these folk carvers regarded during the period

**18** | Eagle, Wilhelm Schimmel, Cumberland Valley, Pennsylvania, 1865–1890 | This artisan referred to his carvings as "fogles," suggesting the German word (*vögel*) for birds. Although presently referred to as eagles, these birds were certainly modeled after Germanic eagles, rather than the more patriotic versions preferred by Americans.

and how widely known was their work? Often the small and simple objects they fashioned (when they were not occupied with farmwork and chores) remained with family and friends; such items were probably not marketed but were given away as tokens of friendship or appreciation, or as toys for young children.

The story of Wilhelm Schimmel's life is not a singular one among creative nineteenth-century artisans, for more than one or two of these talented folk artists died in the almshouses of rural America. Why Schimmel left Germany is unknown, but soon after the Civil War he arrived in Cumberland County, near Carlisle. Schimmel was somewhat of a drifter, working odd jobs, helping farming families with chores, living sometimes in outbuildings, and purportedly charming children with his carvings. In a society where trade and barter were common, his skill in crafting carved objects often earned him food and perhaps all too frequently spirituous drink. His work could be found in local farmhouses as well as local taverns, and this unkempt soul was often seen on the streets of Carlisle in a less than sober state. Not surprisingly, he died a pauper in the Cumberland County Almshouse, and perhaps because he was a well-known character about town, his death was noted in the *Carlisle Evening Sentinel*.[19] Schimmel's eagles as well as the birds and bird trees (fig. 19) wrought by unknown woodcarvers are among the myriad carvings that found their way in the 1920s and 1930s into Henry Francis du Pont's comprehensive collection of Pennsylvania German arts.

Unlike whimsical and ornamental woodcarvings, most of the Pennsylvania German objects collected as art over the past century were originally made to serve very practical functions and might be characterized as useful arts. Iron was forged into great hinges and latches for architectural use or cast for stoves and chimneybacks; brass and copper were fashioned into domestic utensils for cooking and lighting, and tin was made into sconces, candle boxes, and hollowares that were then brilliantly painted. Although blacksmiths performed a multitude of purely utilitarian functions, from shoeing horses to making carriage parts, many of them at their best were brilliantly artful, exhibiting a keen sense of design and whimsy in products both useful and durable. Only rarely did these men of muscle mark or sign their work, but when they did, those objects were almost always worthy of praise.

Evocative of this type of artful yet utilitarian work are the original iron hinges, handle, and latch on a door (fig. 20) made for a church near Lancaster, Pennsylvania, by an anonymous blacksmith. While the iron lock on this door was imported, some complex mechanisms like it were made by local craftsmen. A handsome brass-and-iron lock (fig. 21) was made by David Rohrer (1800–1843) in 1822 and proudly marked "Made By D · Rohrer." Termed a box lock, it would have been used in a house of presumably some

19 | Two figures of birds and a bird tree, attributed to "Schtockschnitzler" (cane carver) Simmons, Berks County, Pennsylvania, 1885 – 1910; Figure of a rooster, attributed to John Reber, Lehigh County, Pennsylvania, about 1880 – 1938 | H. F. du Pont was captivated by the work of known artisans like Schimmel, as well as lesser-known and unknown craftsmen. In the Germanic tradition, birds were depicted not only on fraktur and painted furniture but also in carvings.

**20** | Doors from an eighteenth-century Pennsylvania German church in Lancaster, Pennsylvania | The strongly scrolled iron hinges on this door (now installed in Winterthur's Pottery Alcove) are indicative of Pennsylvania German ironwork and are as artful as they are functional.

**21** | Door lock, David Rohrer, Lebanon, Pennsylvania, 1822 | This box lock is the exception to the rule. Although it would have been equally functional without the decoration, Rohrer engraved the brass with a variety of foliate ornament, including checkered leaves and small round flowers stretching off a vine.

pretension. Like his father John before him, David was an edge-tool maker and locksmith working in Lebanon, Pennsylvania. Rohrer's trade was somewhat specialized, though he also probably made a wide range of hardware. That he signed and dated this special lock 1822 is perhaps significant, for it was in the same year that he purchased his father's shop and tools. Though Rohrer was not a trained engraver, his attempt to ornament the expanse of plain brass on the surface produced a simple but nevertheless charming result.

**22 | Fat lamp, John Long, Lancaster, Pennsylvania, 1848 | John Long's fat lamps are distinctive, for he often engraved both his name and the owner's name on the lamp. Personalization of such a small, utilitarian object was highly unusual, as was the addition of other embellishments: here a finely shaped bird undoubtedly delighted the recipient of the lamp.**

Also fashioned from iron, brass, copper, and tin were a wide variety of lighting devices, ranging from monumental chandeliers often used in public buildings, to functional candlestands and fat lamps. An ancient form used throughout Europe for centuries, the fat lamp was especially popular among settlers of Germanic descent. Metalworkers in eastern Pennsylvania, as well as their clients, embraced this form well into the nineteenth century. The lamp was designed to hang from a hook or a chain by means of the iron pin attached to the top of the curved hook; the light would have emanated from burning the twisted cotton wick, which had been placed in the small reservoir holding fat. Although Pennsylvania fat lamps are often marked, the example at Winterthur (fig. 22) is noteworthy for several reasons. Not only did its maker John Long inscribe his name, the date (1848), and the name of the young woman (Fanny M. Erisman) for whom it was made, but he also added the embellishment of a diminutive brass bird, which is perched on the engraved brass plate. All of this documentation is more easily explained by a custom of the period: traditionally, these fat lamps were presented to young brides as wedding gifts from their parents.[20]

Pennsylvania Germans carried the same penchants for pattern and color from other aspects of their lives into their bedchambers. Their preference for colorful, highly patterned bed coverings is demonstrated by the numerous surviving woven coverlets made by and for them. Germanic cultures made up a bed in a significantly different manner than did those of English background, and not until the mid-nineteenth century did Pennsylvania Germans take up the English convention. One of the primary differences was that instead of the blanket and quilt favored by the English, the Pennsylvania Germans covered themselves with a featherbed and a coverlet. Made most often by professional weavers using cotton and wool provided by the client, these warm and weighty textiles were often given as betrothal or marriage presents. Hence, many have woven into them the name of the weaver, the place where it was produced, the date, and the name of the young person for whom it was made.

Just such a coverlet (fig. 23) was made in 1834 in Lancaster County, not far from the county seat in a small town called New Holland, as stated on the actual textile. The textile also displays the names of the professional who wove it, Isaac Brubaker (d. 1887), and the recipient, E. Ranck—both of whose names suggest good German stock. Brubaker made a patterned, tied double weave called Jacquard after the Frenchman who had invented a loom that could, by using punched cards, create repetitive patterns. The motifs in this coverlet are typical of the vocabulary of ornament brought from Germany with the earliest settlers: stars, tulips, roses, birds, trees, and varied branches of foliage. The same designs appear over and over on different types of utilitarian objects

as well as on presentation (though still "useful") arts. Weavers worked from pattern books, combining various motifs into different patterns reminiscent of German coverlets. Some weavers even owned pattern books published in Germany; Henry Clair of Lancaster County owned *Neues Bild und Muster-Buch* (Heilbronn, 1793), which he inscribed "Bought in August in the Sitty of Lancaster in the year of our Lord Dn 1825 price $5." [21]

One of the earliest surviving examples of an Anglo-American bed covering made by a Pennsylvania German is an embroidered piecework quilt (fig. 24) dated 1830. Though the "E S" who made this quilt is unknown, several other related examples, including one owned by the Moravian Museum in Bethlehem, Pennsylvania, are associated with the Kichline and Schleifer families originally from Bucks County. Therefore, the "E S" quilt was also possibly made by a member of one of those families. The embroidered squares with paired birds and tulips rising out of pots echo motifs seen in numerous fraktur as well as in designs painted on chests and woven into coverlets. Most of the embroidery is worked in crewel wool, however "E S" used her most expensive silk embroidery threads for her initials and the surrounding flowers in the central square and, curiously, for the delicate legs of the birds in the other squares.

23 | Coverlet (corner detail), Isaac Brubaker, New Holland, Lancaster County, Pennsylvania, 1834 | Jacquard coverlets, professionally woven of wool sometimes supplied by the client, often include a corner block that states the maker's or owner's name (here, Isaac Brubaker and E. Ranck) and the date of manufacture (1834).

24 | Quilt (center detail), probably Bucks County, Pennsylvania, 1830 | This quilt, like other utilitarian objects made by Pennsylvania Germans, reflects the merging of English forms (here, the quilt) with Germanic decorative motifs (the fanciful birds).

25 | Spatterware Hall | H. F. du Pont's passion for spatterware led to the creation of an engaging assemblage in a room he appropriately dubbed Spatterware Hall. He artfully lined the walls just beneath the ceiling with gaily decorated saucers and filled various cupboards with an endless variation on this spatterware theme.

Ornamented with designs that echoed the same vocabulary seen on other objects made and owned by Pennsylvania Germans was a type of sponged and often painted English earthenware known by collectors as spatterware.[22] Made principally in the major pottery centers of Staffordshire, England, these wares were presumably marketed in areas of Pennsylvania German settlement, for the high incidence of spatterwares found in these regions suggests that they were eminently affordable and preferred by the Germanic settlers. Sponged and hand-painted on an off-white ground in bright, primary colors, spatterware was decorated with myriad combinations of birds, flowers, stars, houses, vines and berries, and an occasional transfer-printed design such as an eagle and shield. Du Pont's extraordinary installation in Spatterware Hall (fig. 25) on Winterthur's eighth floor suggests that he all but cornered the market on this intriguing pottery.

26 | Cream pots, England, 1810–1860 | This selection illustrates just a few of the combinations of color, form, and ornament that du Pont assiduously collected.

27 | Folk Art Room | Du Pont acquired a number of superb Pennsylvania walnut dressers or cupboards that he filled with quantities of rare, richly decorated sgraffito wares. Originally, these handsome storage pieces would have held primarily utilitarian wares. However, H. F. sought not to imitate their intended use, but rather to create his own aesthetically pleasing installation.

In the early to mid-1920s, as du Pont was furnishing Chestertown House, he had begun to buy quantities of colorful pottery to place in open corner cupboards and broad, straight-fronted dressers. Hattie Brunner was one of du Pont's major sources for pottery, and spatterware was the pottery that caught his fancy. His pursuit of it was almost fanatical: during January alone in 1926 he purchased a total of seventy-seven pieces for the sum of $826. Rows of these cups and shelves lined with plates and pitchers (fig. 26) challenge Spatterware Hall visitors to find any two pieces that are identical.

Equally popular with Pennsylvania Germans were affordable, locally made earthenwares. Eastern Pennsylvania, like other east coast potting regions, had a plentiful amount of iron-rich clay deposits that when fired turned a rich red color; hence, the pottery produced from this material is often called redware. This clay was perfect for forming all sorts of utilitarian wares. Professional potters, many of whom were also farmers, made lead-glazed redwares in a variety of forms serving a wide range of purposes, from eating, drinking, baking, storing, and dairying to personal hygiene. These potters usually worked with one or two family members, and sold their wares within their local region. Fired in wood-fueled kilns, most utilitarian wares were simply glazed without further embellishment or ornamented with "slip" (white clay mixed with water to form a thick, creamy consistency) in a freely applied, decorative manner.

The more highly decorated pottery produced by Pennsylvania German potters is referred to as sgraffito ware because of its scratched, or incised, decoration. This ornament is accomplished by first coating the surface with slip and then incising through the slip the desired decorative motifs or inscriptions. Before firing in the kiln, the overall show surface is highlighted with glazes. The resulting palette is light yellow or buff (the untinted lead glaze over the pale, cream-colored slip), green (copper oxide), and red (where the slip has been scratched or scraped away). These highly ornamental sgraffito wares were among the earliest Pennsylvania German arts to be collected; their first major collector, Edwin AtLee Barber, began about 1900, and Henry Francis du Pont was not far behind, for he began to be seduced by these wares in the 1920s.[23] He acquired a handsome collection of exceptional examples, as demonstrated by the sgraffito wares filling a Pennsylvania walnut dresser (fig. 27) in Winterthur's Pennsylvania Folk Art Room. Although this dresser would have originally held utilitarian pottery, the quantity of richly decorated sgraffito wares displayed in it would not likely have been owned by any one household. But du Pont was not accustomed to understatement, and in his lifetime he managed to assemble a collection of seventy-seven pieces of the coveted scratch-decorated wares. Since his death in 1969 this collection has continued to grow and now includes eighty-one examples, exclusive of the undecorated redwares.

**28** | Plate, Pennsylvania, 1800–1825; Plate, attributed to George Hübener, Montgomery County, Pennsylvania, about 1789; Flowerpot, Pennsylvania, 1810–1840 | Made by Pennsylvania German potters, these two plates and flowerpot represent the wide variety of decoration (from individualized and highly ornate to quite simple) found on sgraffito ware. These pieces fulfilled various needs — functional, decorative, and commemorative.

The names of a number of eighteenth- and nineteenth-century potters are known through actual inscriptions on their work or from various written documents of the period, but signed pieces of sgraffito are rare. Although the plate magnificently decorated with the very Germanic "spread" eagle (fig. 28) is not signed, it is so closely related to one signed by George Hübener and one marked "GH" that an attribution to Hübener is well founded. Like many highly ornamented and inscribed pieces, this plate must have marked a special occasion, for it is inscribed with the date (Merz 5th 1789), the owner's name (Susanna Steltz), and (in German) a saying based on the biblical verse "Do unto others as you would have them do unto you" (Luke 6:31) and the observation that "here is pictured a spread eagle." A very simply decorated, uninscribed plate (fig. 28) shows the other end of the spectrum in terms of ornamentation. Perhaps copying a delftware plate or bowl, this design is simply incised with three stylized fish painted within their outlines with copper oxide. The spare directness of this design has an appeal as stunning as the more highly decorated plate attributed to Hübener.

The Pennsylvania Germans marked the progress of their lives with specially fashioned celebratory objects that were both useful and aesthetically pleasing. They also decorated the items they used every day, from the Rohrer box lock to a simple earthenware flowerpot (fig. 28). It is not surprising that the potter who embellished this object looked to the land for inspiration, for the land was an integral part of their lives, supplying their most basic needs (wood, clay, and food). Given their reliance on the land and all that it provided, they held it in high regard and celebrated it in their arts. As Benjamin Rush instructed the Legislatures of Pennsylvania in 1789, we might all "learn from the history of your German fellow citizens, that you possess an inexhaustible treasure in the bosom of the State, in their manners and arts."[24]

# 5. American Classicism

**Opposite** | Looking glass (detail), New York, 1800–1825 | Dramatically evocative of strong nationalistic sentiments in the early republic, the eagle surmounting this monumental glass typifies Henry Francis du Pont's penchant for acquiring objects with patriotic symbolism.

THROUGHOUT THE SEVENTEENTH AND EIGHTEENTH centuries the basic principles of classicism were taught and practiced by architects and numerous other artists and artisans. Proportion and the classical orders, as set forth by the Roman architect-engineer Vitruvius in the first century BC and then presented by Andrea Palladio (1508–1580) in his *Four Books of Architecture* (1570), were essential points of knowledge for those in the arts. During the second quarter of the eighteenth century in England, Richard Boyle (1694–1753), third earl of Burlington, was the chief proponent of classicism, and even Thomas Chippendale began his *Gentleman and Cabinet-Maker's Director* (London, 1754) with instructions to cabinetmakers on the five classic orders. Although classical proportion and the orders were regarded as essential tenets of design, other tastes prevailed when it came to matters of ornament and style throughout the first three quarters of the eighteenth century.

Intellectually and aesthetically the tide began to turn in the 1740s, when English and European archaeologists and architects began to explore the history of Roman and Grecian cultures as various ancient sites were rediscovered and excavated in Italy and Greece, including the renowned cities of Herculaneum, Pompeii, and Paestum. The material and visual remains that were unearthed excited the modern world and began to shape a different vocabulary of ornament and a new taste. In England, this classical revival was realized by the late 1750s and early 1760s with the return from Italy of

**1** | Du Pont Dining Room |
H. F.'s preference for the
Federal style and patriotic
references prevailed in
this commodiously large
dining room where he fre-
quently entertained in a
manner reflecting his meticulous attention to details,
from the flowers and place
settings, to the menus
served.

Robert Adam (1728–1792) and his brother James (1732–1794). Robert Adam published several influential books, including the *Ruins of the Palace of the Emperor Diocletian at Spalatro in Dalmatia* (1764), which illustrated with detailed drawings his observations abroad. Soon after returning, the Adam brothers began a number of commissions to remodel and update "old-fashioned" houses, such as the sixteenth-century Osterley Park. By the late 1760s and early 1770s, this new style incorporating classical ornament had captured the attention of the cognoscenti in England and the rococo taste soon became passé.

Often referred to as the Adamesque style, this new taste was expressed in spare and slender linear forms, as opposed to the curvilinear shapes of cabriole legs and claw-and-ball feet of the Chippendale (rococo) style. Excavated relics of antiquity inspired both form and ornament, and urns, vases, garlands, rams' heads, and anthemion and acanthus leaves became the cornerstones of this new design vocabulary. The painted wall murals of the ancients inspired new types of interior decoration, as well as extremely sophisticated painted furniture. At Osterley Park, Robert Adam (who often designed interiors and their furnishings in addition to his architectural work) even created an Etruscan Room, a spectacular interpretation of a painted interior with painted furniture to match. Other useful as well as artistic products embodied this new style, and silver tea services were made with urn-shaped bodies and delicate brite-cut engraving with classically inspired garland swags and laurel wreaths. Even such practical objects as chimneybacks and great cast-iron stoves were ornamented with swags, classically draped figures, and anthemion leaves.

How and when did this new style come to the colonies? Often the shift in style and ornament from the Chippendale (rococo) to the early classical is thought to have come about because of America's newly won independence from England: hence, it is often called the Federal style. However, the simultaneous occurrence of the arrival of this style in England and on the Continent, and the beginnings of the move toward American independence was a happy coincidence. Even before the outbreak of the American Revolution, material manifestations of this new style were seen in the colonies.[1] And by the early 1780s, prior to the signing of the Treaty of Paris in 1783, noted artisans and patrons (probably inspired by imported goods) were familiar with this new taste. For instance, such talented artisans as the patriot silversmith Paul Revere (1735–1818) were already producing silver teapots in the newest fashion.[2] By the late 1780s and early 1790s the shape of various forms of furniture had also changed dramatically to reflect the lighter, more linear style. The ornamentation (which often featured light and dark inlays in differing patterns) was usually as restrained as the forms it decorated.

Although H. F. du Pont's greatest love was the rococo style, he nevertheless fully embraced this early classical (Federal) style in one of his most important and oft used rooms, the Du Pont Dining Room (fig. 1). That he inherited his family's set of square-back New York side chairs (made about 1790–1800), which he had grown up with, may have compelled him to design his grand eating room in this style. But du Pont's interest in the Federal style was perhaps more integrally tied to an intense sense of nationalism and reverence for Revolutionary heroes and the leaders of America's early republic. To set forth this patriotic theme in his dining room, du Pont prominently displayed over the chimneybreast Gilbert Stuart's likeness of George Washington, one of the many replicas of the so-called Vaughan portrait. And he installed a Baltimore dining table that has inlaid ovals containing eagles at the top of each leg. Such eagle-inlay motifs, emblematic of the newly proclaimed republic and echoing the great seal of the United States (adopted in 1782), were highly sought after by collectors in the early twentieth century. H. F. himself amassed many pieces of eagle-inlaid furniture, including card tables, pembroke tables, sideboards, and dining tables. Du Pont carried the dining room's nationalistic theme even further by placing Bohemian glassware engraved with the great seal on the top of the Baltimore table.

In 1926 du Pont acquired one of his most outstanding examples of early classical cabinetwork: a great New York sideboard that he placed in the Du Pont Dining Room once his addition to the original house was complete in 1931 (in 1929, when he lent this sideboard to the landmark *Girl Scouts Loan Exhibition* in New York, it was a focal point in the Federal gallery).[3] For the past seven decades, this impressive sideboard, along with the extraordinary objects du Pont placed on and above it, has stood as a monument to both early classicism and the heroes of our republic (figs. 2, 3). In 1928 du Pont acquired an extraordinarily rare set of six tankards fashioned in 1772 by Paul Revere (the widow Mary Bartlett had commissioned them as a gift to the Third Church in Brookfield, Massachusetts). These tankards were appropriately placed atop this richly veneered sideboard along with two monumental urn-shaped knife cases originally owned by millionaire merchant Elias Hasket Derby (1739–1799) and a selection of exquisite pieces of Chinese porcelain made for the American market. This impressive grouping is one of Henry Francis du Pont's most brilliant tributes not only to the newly adopted classical style, but also to America's hard-won independence.

Over this patriotic display, du Pont hung Benjamin West's unfinished painting (figs. 2, 3) of the American commissioners who traveled to Paris in November 1782 for the initial peace negotiations with the British. Though Benjamin West (1738–1820) spent most of his mature career in England and received significant patronage from the court of

**2** | *American Commissioners of the Preliminary Peace Negotiations with Great Britain* (detail), Benjamin West, London, 1783–1784 | Benjamin Franklin, one of the five American statesmen sent to Paris to discuss the preliminary articles of peace following the Revolution, numbered Benjamin West among his friends.

George III, he was a native-born Pennsylvanian who had grown up in the Delaware Valley just west of Philadelphia. He traveled to Italy in 1760 to study classical art and after three years, he settled in London, where he became one of America's most well-known expatriate artists. By the 1770s West was fully engaged in the depiction of major historical subjects, including relatively contemporary events. He desired, as he wrote his friend Charles Willson Peale in the summer of 1783, to paint a series of pictures around the subject of the Revolutionary War. West's *American Commissioners* (1783−1784) was a noble effort. However, he failed to complete it because (as West related to John Quincy Adams) the British representative, Richard Oswald, refused to sit for his portrait. Adams later wrote in his diary, "Mr. Oswald, the British Plenipotentiary, was an ugly looking man, blind of one eye, and he died without leaving any picture of him extant. This Mr. West alledged as the cause which prevented him from finishing the picture many years ago."[4] Hence, West was left with an unfinished sketch of five important statesmen who appear to be in the midst of a pleasant conversation, as opposed to a difficult peace negotiation. Four of those pictured actually sat for West in London from 1783 to 1784; on the far left are John Jay (standing) and John Adams (seated), and on the right, Henry Laurens (standing) and William Temple Franklin (seated). His grandfather, Benjamin Franklin himself (seated in the middle) did not go to London after the negotiations, and West had to take his likeness from the well-known portrait by French artist Joseph Siffred Duplessis. West may well have intended to paint a larger version of this sketch (had it been completed), and Adams wrote in his diary that "I understand his intention to be to make a present of it to Congress." But the unfinished canvas remained in West's hands, and after his death it was sold at auction in London to an Englishman in whose family it remained until purchased in 1916 by J. Pierpont Morgan Jr. In 1944 du Pont acquired it from Knoedler Galleries in New York.[5]

By the time the Treaty of Paris was signed in 1783 and American independence was recognized, wealthy, fashion-conscious citizens (some newly rich from wartime ventures) once again traveled abroad, shopping and immersing themselves in all the latest trends and styles of England and Europe. In addition, emigré artisans settling in America sought opportunities in urban centers such as Baltimore, where war had not economically devastated the marketplace. Baltimore was the youngest, fastest-growing port city on the eastern seaboard at the end of the Revolution. Since the harbor at Baltimore had never been blockaded during the war, vessels were able to collect grain, foodstuffs, and other varied supplies from the fertile farmlands of the interior states north and west of the city. Hence, great profits accrued to the new merchant class, which demanded the most up-to-date household articles (both imported and locally

3 | Du Pont Dining Room, north wall | Du Pont's assemblage of singularly important and aesthetically significant objects is a tour de force of the Federal style: a most magnificent New York sideboard, six silver tankards by Paul Revere, urn-shaped knife boxes ordered by one of New England's richest merchants, and Benjamin West's historic *American Commissioners*, which appropriately hangs opposite Gilbert Stuart's portrait of George Washington.

made) to appoint its many fashionable new residences. American collectors have long recognized the extraordinary accomplishments of Baltimore artisans, but only recently has the full extent of the English contribution to the design aesthetic of the postwar production in that area been totally realized.[6] Although at least 80 percent of the approximately thirty cabinetmakers were native born, the influence of English style and taste was nevertheless pervasive. Emigré artisans, imported design sources and objects, and patrons' travels abroad greatly aided in this transferal of style.

4 | Ladies desk, Baltimore, 1790–1810; Side chair, Baltimore, 1790–1810 | The wealth of Baltimore, the youngest and fastest-growing port city on the eastern seaboard by the 1780s, provided for the creation of elaborate pieces of early classical furniture whose reverse-painted and gilt glass panels and shaded wood inlay echo ancient forms.

The overall form of the diminutive and delicately proportioned ladies dressing cabinet and writing desk (fig. 4) is intrinsically English, yet it speaks with a Maryland accent. Derived from drawings published by the English designer Thomas Sheraton in his *Cabinet-maker and Upholsterer's Drawing-Book* (London, 1791–1793), this unusual piece appears to be a combination of two separate designs, plate 49 for "A Lady's Cabinet Dressing Table" and plate 50 for "A Lady's Cabinet and Writing Table." The unique embellishment in the upper section of five oval glass panels, painted and gilt on the reverse with classically garbed figures, is a manner of ornamentation favored by Baltimore patrons. Reverse-painted glass panels picturing urns and twisted vine motifs (executed in a technique called églomisé) flank the drawers in the lower section in much the same manner as inlaid ornament might have. Satinwood veneer surrounds the églomisé ovals and elevates the aesthetic expression as well as the cost. Equally indicative of Baltimore styles and preferences is an elegant heart-back side chair with eagle inlay (fig. 4).[7] Although this shape was also produced in the other mid-Atlantic urban centers of Philadelphia and New York, Baltimore patrons had a special fondness for the added ornament of eagle inlay (perhaps because they could afford, and wanted, more embellishment).

Citizens of the new republic living in less urban areas of New England were nevertheless abreast of current fashions and equally as patriotic, even though their expressions of nationalism differed. Connecticut artist Ralph Earl, who (following an eight-year stay in England) painted many well-to-do and prominent citizens of the Connecticut River valley, executed this glowing image (fig. 5) of eighteen-year-old Jerusha Benedict of Danbury in 1790. Typical of many of Earl's likenesses, this charming painting suggests the burgeoning refinement of the upper middle class from which young Jerusha came. Perhaps using conventions derived from English conversation pieces he may have seen, Earl seated young Jerusha outside in a green painted windsor chair; a bird (perhaps a pet) perches on a highly polished stand beside her, while the large white house in the distant landscape may allude to her family's abode, no doubt a commodious structure since her father, Zadock Benedict, had founded the lucrative

**5** | *Jerusha Benedict*, Ralph Earl, Danbury, Connecticut, 1790 | Like many of the Connecticut River valley residents Earl painted in the early 1790s, young Jerusha, the daughter of an early industrialist, is emblematic of increasing refinement among the upper middle class in post-Revolutionary America. In 1792, she married Isaac Ives, a Yale graduate and a lawyer in Danbury.

**6** | Tambour desk, John Seymour and Son, Boston, 1794–1804 | This labeled writing desk represents one of the new forms that became popular as styles changed in the late eighteenth century. Tambour refers to the manner in which the doors are constructed: thin strips of wood (usually veneered) are glued on canvas so that they slide open, curving around the sides of the desk and across the back.

hat industry in Danbury, Connecticut. Jerusha's hat, hairstyle, and elegant dress are all indicative of rapidly changing fashions in the early 1790s.

New England's oldest urban center was Boston, which remained relatively conservative both in taste and economic prowess during much of the second half of the eighteenth century. However, by the 1790s another generation of both patrons and artisans began to change the milieu of this major port city. Federal Boston, as well as her neighboring northern cities of Salem, Massachusetts, and Portsmouth, New Hampshire, embraced the new, classically inspired fashions at least as fully as any other place. Responding to the demands of clients with both old money as well as new capital from recently opened trading ventures (such as those with China), craftsmen produced regionally distinctive and finely crafted material possessions. While some Boston artisans represented generations of native New Englanders, others had recently come to these shores seeking new opportunities. Among the latter was the English-born cabinetmaker John Seymour (1738–1818?), who in 1784 came from Devonshire in southeastern England to Portland, Maine, and in 1793, to Boston. Because Seymour labeled a number of his pieces, his name, as well as that of his son Thomas, has long been acknowledged in the annals of admired American craftsmanship. However, only in the past few years has major research into his English background, as well as his Portland and Boston associations, been thoroughly explored.[8]

The tambour desk (fig. 6) is one of thirteen documented examples of the work of John Seymour and his son Thomas. Dramatically different from the Baltimore ladies desk (fig. 4), this desk is nonetheless an excellent example of a parallel Boston form presumably also made for use by a lady.[9] The quality of materials selected, the level of design and

technical execution, and the resulting delicacy of expression all contribute to making this piece a primary example of the work of this provincially trained artisan. Of particular note is the handling of the bell-flower swag inlay on the face of the tambour (or reeded) doors of the upper case. Du Pont acquired this labeled example in January 1930 at the sale of the noted collection of Philip Flayderman,[10] even though he already owned a similar tambour desk (which he had lent to the 1929 *Girl Scouts Loan Exhibition*).[11] No doubt his keen eye and desire to possess superior documented examples by known craftsmen made the Boston desk an irresistible acquisition.

The Boston that John Seymour and his family moved to in 1793 was an urbane and highly sophisticated city, and Mrs. Perez Morton (fig. 7) was at the apex of its high-toned society. A charming, well-born woman with a good mind and a talent with the pen, Sarah Wentworth Apthorp Morton was descended from notable New England merchants and political leaders. In 1781 she married Perez Morton, who had been born into an equally old Massachusetts family, graduated from Harvard, and served in the Revolution. Together they were key participants in the culturally and intellectually poised new Federal elite. A published poet, Sarah Morton was dubbed "the American Sappho" by critic Thomas Paine. Winterthur's provocative portrait of this charming poet is one of three Gilbert Stuart painted of her when she and her husband were visiting Philadelphia in 1802.[12] Stuart not only aptly captured the beauty of this elegant woman, but he also seeded the portrait with suitable symbols suggestive of her accomplishments and position. The richly upholstered, gilt-framed armchair she sits in might well be an imported English or French piece of furniture signifying a level of taste only the affluent could support. Her gold and pearl jewelry reinforces this economic situation, while the papers and inkstand allude to her accomplishments as a published writer. The bust of Washington in the background is a subtle but significant reminder that the Mortons were his friends and admirers. Indeed, in 1798 Sarah had sent Washington an inscribed copy of "Beacon Hill" (a poem she wrote in 1797 on the Revolution), addressing it "To George Washington, A Name honored in History — / Loved by the Muses — / and immortal as Memory — / The following poem originated by Enthusiasm, / is presented with Diffidence from The Author."

Honored, loved, and immortal are three words that most certainly best describe how Americans felt about General Washington. Soon after the end of the war, and the signing of the Treaty of Paris in 1783, representations glorifying Washington and others, such as Franklin, were produced for consumption by not only the affluent but also the masses. Depicting heroic personages in the context of allegorical figures was common practice in the eighteenth century. Hence, figures such as Liberty, Peace, Fame

**7** | *Mrs. Perez Morton (Sarah Wentworth Apthorp)*, Gilbert Stuart, Philadelphia, 1802–1803 | Known for her 1790 poem *Ouabi; or, The Virtues of Nature, an Indian Tale,* Sarah Morton held a position of great social and cultural status in Boston. Gilbert Stuart referenced her literary talent by including her books; her fine dress and jewelry indicate her wealth and stature.

as a trumpeting angel, America as an Indian in feathered headdress, and Commerce with bundles of produce were especially appropriate symbols to celebrate the nation's newly won independence and to deify those heroes who had made it happen. By 1784 and 1785 furnishing fabrics printed with patriotic themes were readily available for eager Americans who wished to (and could afford to) enshrine their parlors and bedchambers with images of America's most famous.

The English copperplate-printed textile depicting the "Apotheosis of Benjamin Franklin and George Washington" (fig. 8) was available and in use in this country by 1785. Young Tommy Shippen of Philadelphia visited New York in 1785, staying in the President's House with his uncle, Richard Henry Lee, then president of the Congress. The impressionable lad was duly struck by what he termed a "Palace"; he wrote from his

**8** | Plate-printed cotton (detail), England, 1785–1790 | English furnishing fabrics such as this copperplate-printed design honoring George Washington and Benjamin Franklin were available in America soon after the Revolution ended. Depicting heroic personages in the context of allegorical figures was a common practice in the eighteenth century.

"spacious…elegant…and prettily furnished" bedchamber that "which way soever I turn my eyes I find a triumphal Car, a Liberty Cap, a Temple of Fame or the Hero of Heroes [Washington], all these and many more objects of a piece with them, being finely represented on the hangings."[13] This fabric was apparently exceedingly popular in America and was produced in red, purple, blue, and brown (shown) so that a wide choice was available for the color-conscious consumer. Images of famous heroes depicted on furnishing fabrics were usually copied from widely circulated prints that were engraved after paintings.

Just as his ancestors must have admired Washington, H. F. was no less enamored of the great man: he assembled many objects and paintings honoring and depicting Washington. The wartime experience of living and fighting for freedom and liberty under the command of such a person as Washington bred a devotion and camaraderie amongst his officers (akin to classical hero worship) that was quickly recognized in a special way. In 1783, under the direction of both Washington and Henry Knox, the Society of the Cincinnati was formed, uniting those officers who had served under Washington in the Revolution. This honorary society derived its name from an appropriately classical personage, the famous fifth-century Roman farmer turned military leader, Cincinnatus. Thomas Jefferson recollected that the idea for this organization had originated in 1776 when Washington and several of his generals, including Knox, were dining at a tavern in the state of New York. In talking of ancient history and the Romans, Knox mentioned that "he would wish for some ribbon to wear in his hat or in his button hole, to be transmitted to his descendants as a badge and a proof that he had fought in defense of their liberties."[14] At the first meeting of the society it was decided that the insignia should incorporate the bald eagle, the figure of Cincinnatus, and the classical figure of fame. Maj. Pierre-Charles L'Enfant, chief engineer for the army and also the architect-designer for the new nation, was asked to procure in Paris the membership certificates and eagle badges, made of gold with enamel decoration (fig. 9). Today some of these original badges remain in the families of descendants of Washington's Revolutionary officers, but others have become rare and prized possessions of collectors like Henry Francis du Pont.

In addition to the very desirable and collectable original gold badges given to the members of the society, pieces from Washington's Cincinnati dinner service were also sought by many early collectors (as they are by collectors today). Du Pont was no exception, but the quantity that he was able to amass was exceptional! With the beginning of direct trade between the new republic and China in 1784, it is not surprising that Chinese export porcelain dinner and tea wares painted with the insignia of the Society

**9** | Order of the Society of the Cincinnati badge, Paris, 1783–1800 | Presented to officers who had served under George Washington in the Revolutionary War, these gold badges with enamel decoration signified membership in an honored society of those who had proudly defended freedom and liberty.

**10** | Covered tureen, platter, and dinner plate, China, 1784 | Painted with the insignia of the Society of the Cincinnati by special order in China, this service consisted of 302 pieces and was purchased by George Washington.

of the Cincinnati were ordered (fig. 10). The first of four known groups of this prized porcelain to be brought back from the Orient was commissioned by Samuel Shaw, himself a founding member of the society, a former aide-de-camp to General Knox, and the supercargo on the *Empress of China* (which sailed from New York in February 1784). Having a FitzHugh type border, this service (fig. 10) was purchased by Washington through his friend and former officer Henry (Light-Horse Harry) Lee. A little over a year after the ship's return, Henry Lee wrote to Washington from New York: "If you should be in want of a new set of china it is in my power to procure a very gentele set, table & tea—What renders this china doubly valuable & handsome is the order of the eagle engraved on it, in honor of the Cincinnati." The original invoice for this service noted "1 Sett of Cincinnati China Contg, 1 Breakfast, 1 Table, 1 Tea Service of 302 ps.," an enormous number of pieces for the sum of £60.[15]

Elected unanimously as the first president of the United States of America on 30 April 1789, George Washington was sworn into office in New York City, then the capital of the new republic. Many unspoken challenges faced the fifty-six-year-old hero, and while he was well suited to accept them, he nevertheless feared he could not meet them adequately. Earlier that April he had written to a friend that "my movements to the chair of Government will be accompanied by feelings not unlike those of a culprit who is going to his place of execution; so unwilling am I, in the evening of a life nearly consumed in public cares, to quit a peaceful Abode for an Ocean of difficulties, without that competency of political skill — abilities & inclination which is necessary to manage the helm."[16] Well aware of the untrodden ground that lay ahead, Washington was often frustrated — even angered — at the process, or lack of precedent for process. For example, one of the first matters that Washington faced was one of great diplomatic delicacy: a treaty with the southern Creek tribe of Indians in August of 1789.[17] Among the material reminders of these negotiations that have survived today are the silver peace medals (fig. 11) that were given to Indian chiefs and other distinguished members of the tribe. The earliest medals were made in 1789, in Philadelphia and presumably in New York City; a later series was made in Philadelphia (then the seat of government) by 1792. Engraved on one side with the great seal of the United States and on the other with an emblematic image of peacemaking, these medals were worn with great pride around the necks of those to whom they were presented. Interestingly, the Indians objected to the depiction of an Indian and allegorical female warrior sharing the peace pipe (as on the 1789 medal). On later peace medals, the image was changed to show a male figure holding the pipe with the Indian.[18]

Although various artists painted Washington as the famed commander-in-chief of the Continental Army, perhaps no image is as correct and insightful as Col. John Trumbull's 1790 painting (fig. 12) of the general reviewing the French troops at Verplanck's Point in 1782. Painted as a gift to Martha Washington from the artist, it hung in the New Room (Banqueting Room) at Mount Vernon, where George Washington Parke Custis, Martha's grandson, remembers it. Custis remarked in his *Recollections of Washington* that "The figure of Washington, as delineated by Colonel Trumbull, is the most perfect extant."[19]

The young artist and his family knew Washington well. Trumbull's father was the governor of Connecticut during the war and a loyal friend of Washington's, and the artist himself served with the forces as an aide-de-camp to the general. This familiarity certainly gave Trumbull access to the general upon the artist's return from studying and painting in London in 1789–1790. Trumbull was working on several large historical canvases showing American victories and needed a likeness of Washington. The gen-

**11** | Medal (obverse and reverse), Joseph Richardson Jr., Philadelphia, 1789 | Presented to chiefs and other prominent Indians, these peace medals recognized the amicable treaty negotiations between the American government and various tribes.

**12** | *Washington at Verplanck's Point*, John Trumbull, New York, 1790 | Not only is this portrait one of the best-known images of the great general in Revolutionary uniform, but at the time it was also reputed to be one of the most perfect likenesses ever taken of Washington.

eral, upon seeing them, was taken with Trumbull's abilities and granted him at least fourteen sittings in the first half of 1790. Custis recalls that "the painter had *standings* as well as sittings—the white charger, fully caparisoned, having been led out and held by a groom." The artist was meticulous in his observations, as well as in bringing to this representation a personal, firsthand intimacy with Washington. It is no surprise then that he so ably captured the figure and face of this hero.

Although Washington loved Mount Vernon and his life there, his military service and two terms as president left him little time to be the farmer (Cincinnatus) he so deeply wished to be. When he was along the Potomac, his domestic life centered around looking after the many aspects of his more than eight thousand acres and fostering stepchildren (Martha had two children from a previous marriage and later two grandchildren). Though Washington had no children of his own, by all accounts he was an excellent father to these children. His days began with the sunrise and ended about nine in the evening, with much time spent keeping up his voluminous correspondence. However,

**13** | *The Washington Family*, Edward Savage, United States, about 1798 | This endearing image of the nation's first "first family" was also engraved and became enormously popular with numerous Americans, who displayed the print in their homes to pay homage to the great hero.

he undoubtedly enjoyed some quiet familial moments like those depicted (albeit stiffly) by Edward Savage in his *Washington Family* of about 1798 (fig. 13). Surprisingly, this work is the only contemporary illustration that was ever done of the nation's first "first family" at Mount Vernon. Savage had this image engraved upon its completion, and it was an instant success with the public when it reached their hands and walls.[20]

The Washingtons entertained constantly at Mount Vernon; guests were often close friends but sometimes they were admirers who hardly knew the couple but who had come to meet and pay homage to the famous leader and hero. Gifts were frequently brought to the general, but a very unique group of china (fig. 14) came as a gift to Martha Washington in 1796 from a Dutchman and great admirer of hers, Andreas Everardus van Braam Houckgeest (1739–1801). Van Braam had been director of Canton operations for the Dutch East India Company from 1790–1795, and in 1796 he arrived in Philadelphia, where he settled until he returned to Europe in 1798; he died in Amsterdam in 1801. The "Box of China for Lady Washington" that arrived in Philadelphia in the ship *Lady Louisa* in April 1796 was most likely designed by Van Braam, though he obviously drew heavily upon contemporary printed material of his day.[21] The set is often referred to as the "States" china; the rim is circled with a "chain of states," the whole of which is contained within a blue serpent signifying the eternal circle. Martha's initials are conjoined on a gold disc with a gold sunburst above and a red banner beneath. The motto in the banner, which translates to "A glory and defense from it," was adapted from Vergil's *Aeneid* (an appropriate classical allusion to a protective breastplate he called a "defense in battle"). Apparently, Van Braam intended a reference to the defensive strength of the states in their new union.

**14** | Plate, China, 1795–1796 | Specially designed as a gift for Martha Washington, this plate is part of a larger service commissioned by a Dutchman (and friend of the Washingtons) who was director of Canton operations for the Dutch East India Company prior to his settling in Philadelphia.

Refusing to run for a third term as president, Washington returned to Mount Vernon in 1797, probably hoping to spend many more years there than fate was to grant him. On 14 December 1799 he died, having taken ill two days earlier after being caught in a winter storm while reviewing his farms. As news of the great man's passing rippled through the nation, a tremendous sorrow gripped a united America. Expressions of mourning included both the usual, such as rings and various other pieces of jewelry, and the unusual, such as the mock funeral held by the citizens of Philadelphia twelve days after his death.[22] Certainly one of the most popular customs at the time was the making of silk embroidered needlework mourning pictures, and this national event occasioned numerous examples. Embellished with classical imagery, these were usually made by women family members for deceased loved ones; but since all considered Washington a "father" (the patriarch of the American people), numbers of these mementoes were wrought by women throughout the nation.

**15** | Needlework picture, E.S. Sefford, United States, 1800–1810 | Based on similar contemporary prints, such needlework mourning pieces served as a means for Americans to express their profound grief at the death of George Washington. This remarkable example has survived with its original reverse-painted glass and gilt frame.

**16** | Clock, Jean-Baptiste Dubuc, Paris, 1804–1817 | Capitalizing on America's craze for objects honoring its heroes, various French manufacturers created clocks depicting Washington (or other great men such as Benjamin Franklin or Lafayette) for the American market.

Memorial needlework pictures in memory of Washington embraced a wide range of expressions and abilities. One (fig. 15) made by "E.S. SEFFORD" is particularly exceptional both in quality of design as well as execution. Typically, early nineteenth-century mourning pictures have as a basic element a weeping willow tree and a tomb monument of some form. In Sefford's work, she chose a white obelisk, with an oval watercolor portrait bust of Washington applied to its face. A weeping soldier stands at the right of the tomb, with weeping female figures to the left and right, and angels trumpeting him heavenward. The inscription on the face of the tomb reads "Sacred to the Memory of the truly illustrious George Washington, Renown'd in War, Great in the senate, & possessed of every Qualification to render him worth the Title of Great and Good."

Memorials to Washington continued even after the immediacy of his death had passed. For decades, even centuries, Americans have remembered him, placing his image—a type of immortality—on everything from the one dollar bill to rare and valued objects like portrait miniatures and even timepieces. One such example is the French mantel clock (fig. 16) that Jean-Baptiste Dubuc, an eminent Parisian artisan, made particularly for the American market sometime during the two decades following Washington's death. Crowned with the patriotic symbol of the eagle, the clock is flanked by the more mundane surveying instruments (spyglass and protractor) Washington used in his pursuits prior to the Revolution and by the figure of Washington himself, who stands heroically to one side with sword in one hand and his resignation as commander-in-chief of the Continental Army in the other. The drapery beneath the clock face bears the now-famous quotation from Maj. Gen. Henry Lee's funeral oration: "Washington: First in War, First in Peace, and First in the Hearts of his Countrymen." The plaque in the center of the lower section depicts the great man receiving a sword from the head of state, a direct reference to the Roman farmer turned soldier, Cincinnatus. Undoubtedly timepieces of this quality and stature were costly items even in the period when they were made, hence they were highly prized and regarded by their fortunate owners. Joseph B. Barry (1759–1838), a noted Philadelphia cabinetmaker, made specific reference to "the Washington Clock" that he owned when he made his will and left it to his daughter, Ann Barry.[23] The Philadelphia silversmiths Simon Chaudron and Thomas Fletcher both imported and sold French mantel clocks, amongst which were probably ones memorializing our nation's hero.

By the first decade of the nineteenth century (not long after Washington's death), the light and linear early classical style, which had drawn its inspiration primarily from English precedents and particularly the work of those following the lead of Robert Adam, was eclipsed by a more robust and curvilinear classical style. Drawing heavily on Napoleonic French design precedents, this later style is characterized as more archaeologically correct, for it followed more directly the forms and ornament of ancient objects unearthed, studied, and drawn in Italy and, eventually, in Greece. Although du Pont was quite enamored of the early classical (Federal) style, purchasing numerous pieces in the late 1920s and early 1930s, he was not attracted to later classical (Empire) pieces. No doubt his reason for not initially being drawn to the Empire style stemmed from the fact that he had grown up with much of it. Years later he explained, "As my only acquaintance with American mahogany was with the Empire veneered variety which had been in the home of my family and which I heartily disliked, I decided we would not have a piece of it at Southampton."[24]

But in 1930, as he was building his most major addition to Winterthur, he purchased fourteen pieces of furniture from New York collector Louis Guerineau Myers; eleven of these objects were in the later classical style and attributed to the famed Scottish emigré cabinetmaker Duncan Phyfe (1768–1856). Du Pont soon began to appreciate what other collectors had already recognized as a very compelling style, for he wrote to Myers about the eleven pieces, "Your Phyfe looks beautiful and I must say that for a long while I could not see Phyfe. Its charm, however, does grow on one more and more as time goes on."[25] And by 1931 he had created a Phyfe Room (fig. 17), where the original eleven were joined by a set he acquired in 1931: ten side chairs and two armchairs (fig. 17) that were accompanied by their original bill of 1807 from Phyfe to wealthy New York merchant William Bayard (1761–1826).[26] It was not until 1938 that he purchased appropriate woodwork for this large and handsomely appointed room. But the wait was well worth it, for the mantelpiece and moldings were originally installed at No. 7 State Street, New York, the home of Moses Rogers. William Bayard at No. 6 State Street was Rogers' next-door neighbor.

The form of the armchair (fig. 17) and its accompanying side chairs was referred to as a scroll-back chair in period sources such as price books; it was also called a Grecian chair contemporaneously.[27] Almost all of the design features of the armchair can be traced to Greek or Roman precedents, as can the ornamental carving of thunderbolts tied in the center with a ribbon across the scrolled back crest-rail. While the overall form and the carved ornament is often associated with the large and productive workshop of Duncan Phyfe, numerous other artisans in New York City undoubtedly also produced

**17 | Phyfe Room, north wall |** During the early 1930s du Pont assembled a group of various forms of New York classical-style furniture attributed to the renowned Scottish emigré cabinetmaker Duncan Phyfe. The armchair on the right (one of a pair) is from an important set of ten side chairs and two armchairs made in 1807 for New York merchant William Bayard. Accompanied by the original bill from Phyfe, the set was acquired by du Pont in 1931.

**18** | *Victorine du Pont,* Rembrandt Peale, near Wilmington, Delaware, 1813 | In this classically inspired portrait, Peale captured the aura of the period: the sitter's clothing, pose, hairstyle, and *klismos* chair all represent the prevailing Grecian taste of the early nineteenth century.

**19** | Plate 24, from *A series of twenty-nine designs of modern costume,* Henry Moses (London, 1823) | Illustrations like those published by Henry Moses informed young Americans not only of current styles of dress and furnishings, but also of fashionable entertainments.

this form and ornament. Chairs of this type were also made as legitimate reproductions late in the nineteenth century, and often they are so skillfully executed that they are difficult to discern from true late classical period examples.[28]

Henry Francis du Pont's French ancestors clearly embraced this late classical style in the first few decades of their residency in America. The evocative portrait (fig. 18) of twenty-one-year-old Victorine du Pont (1792–1861), painted by Rembrandt Peale (1778–1860) in 1813, evokes the classical serenity indicative of portraiture at that time. The eldest of four daughters of Eleuthère Irenée du Pont (the first du Pont to come to America and the founder of the Dupont Company), Victorine was the older sister of Evelina, who would eventually marry James Antoine Bidermann and become the first owner and builder of Winterthur. Emblematic of the prevailing classical taste in the early nineteenth century is her gauze-like white "Greek dress" with short puffy sleeves, low neckline, and high waist pulled in tightly below the bustline. Her simple hairdo with romantic ringlets falling across her face and the red shawl draped over the tablet top of a Grecian chair both reinforce the stylish aura of this very classical portrait.[29] Even her pose (she is seated almost sideways in the chair with her arm resting casually on the edge of the chair's tablet top) typifies the more relaxed postures adopted by young women as they daringly donned these revealing dresses with neither stays nor stomachers. That Rembrandt Peale had visited Paris twice at the end of the first decade of the nineteenth century—where he would have had the opportunity to study the paintings of French artists such as Jacques-Louis David (1748–1825), then immersed in the classical Napoleonic style of the day—is an important factor in the nature of his subsequent work in America. In Victorine's portrait he decidedly drew upon his recent exposure to French classicism as he rendered this sensitive and fashionable image of a young French woman in America.

In the later classical style, the direct influence of French design upon the English and their subsequent publications can be readily seen in both singular sources like Thomas Hope's influential *Household Furniture and Interior Decoration* (London, 1807) and George Smith's *A Collection of Designs for Household Furniture* (London, 1808), as well as more widely distributed popular monthly magazines like Rudolph Ackermann's *The Repository of Arts,*... Other illustrated books that informed fashion-conscious Americans about the latest vogues abroad included Henry Moses' *A series of twenty-nine designs of modern costume* (London, 1823), which details fashionable dress and entertainments (fig. 19). Such publications not only showed the most current styles of dress and furnishing interiors, but also suggested the postures that one might assume when sitting in or standing about this very sensuous, curvilinear furniture.

**20** | *Klismos* side chair (one of a pair), Baltimore, 1815–1825 | The most expensive and sophisticated Grecian-style chairs produced in Baltimore were also closest to the ancient prototypes (called *klismos* in Greek) that they imitated. The taste for brilliantly painted and decorated furniture was especially prevalent in this rapidly growing center of wealth and commerce.

One of the first manifestations of seating furniture in the later classical style was the New York scroll-back chair (see fig. 17), but it was not long before more full-blown Grecian (so-called *klismos*) chairs with broad, curving tablet tops such as those seen in Henry Moses' illustrations were being made in most major urban centers. Philadelphia and Boston chairmakers in particular produced very dramatically designed mahogany *klismos* chairs with deeply swept rear stiles and bold tablet tops. Beginning about 1800 the fashion for imported English painted seating furniture (in the major urban centers along the east coast) spurred American makers to compete with this trend. Since Baltimore was a rapidly growing, wealthy city, the preference for this fashionable furniture was stronger there than in any other urban area. Today the surviving legacy of Baltimore painted furniture stands as a distinctive regional expression. A painted *klismos* chair (fig. 20), one of a pair at Winterthur, is among the finer surviving examples of this distinctive Baltimore production. The brilliantly executed painting of paired griffins and foliate scrolls across the tablet top is representative of the work of the most talented Baltimore fancy painters and might well be from the shop of Hugh and John Finlay, the most notable artisans of their day. With most of the forms and ornament drawn "from the stores of antiquity"[30] this classical painted furniture is today among the most desirable as well as the rarest.

Seating furniture of this period, especially Baltimore painted furniture, was sometimes made in large suites that included pairs of card tables, pier tables, and perhaps even a center table.[31] A red painted Baltimore card table (fig. 21) is one of the most elaborate and well-preserved examples to come to light in recent years. The design convention of the romantic, imaginary landscape with classical ruins in an oval in the center of the skirt (and in half ovals at the rear sides) is seen on other Baltimore card and pier tables. Though no seating forms or matching card tables from this suite are known, a matching pier table was owned by Andy Warhol,[32] but unfortunately no provenance exists for either of these pieces that could help identify the original owners and houses for which they were made. The square tapered legs with a distinctive outward curve at the bottom are unusual, but the leaf and berry ornament on the legs is seen on another important suite of furniture that is believed to have been made in Philadelphia, but decorated in Baltimore by Hugh and John Finlay.[33] The brilliant red paint, resembling Chinese lacquerwork, and the delicate gold lattice design on the skirt lend a chinoiserie taste to this superior piece of Baltimore painted furniture. A complete suite of such extraordinarily sophisticated furniture would have been quite impressive in a great saloon or assembly room used for festive gatherings.

**21** | Card table, Baltimore, 1800–1810 | An extraordinary survival representing some of the finest Baltimore furniture, this painted red card table has a dense mahogany top leaf: when open, the playing surface is a brilliant red with gold decorative designs (see detail above).

**22, 23** | Vase (left), Josiah Wedgwood's Factory, Staffordshire, England, 1790 –1800; Ewer (right), Thomas Fletcher and Sidney Gardiner, Philadelphia, 1812 – 1820 | Decorative and useful forms echoing those from the annals of antiquity proliferated both abroad and in America from the years following the Revolution until well into the nineteenth century. Especially popular was the vase (or urn) shape seen here in both an imported ceramic and an American-made silver form.

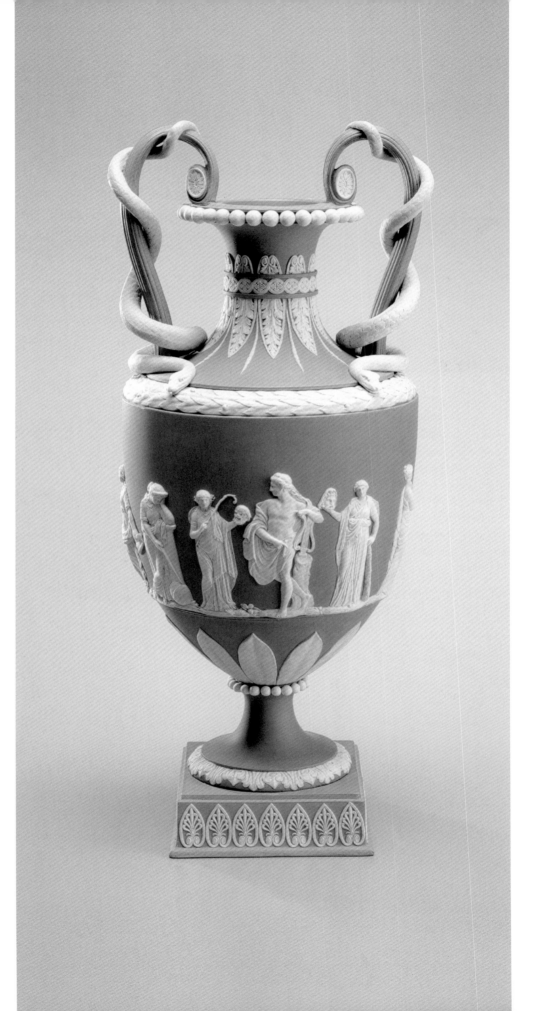

Designers and artisans of late classical objects used a vast vocabulary of form and ornament drawn from the ancient past that included urn forms, classically draped figures of Greek gods and goddesses, acanthus leaves, paw feet, snakes, and dolphins. Imported objects from both France and England often served as inspiration for American patrons and craftsmen once these pieces were located in prominent domestic settings. Among the types of wares that can be documented as being in America toward the end of the eighteenth and early nineteenth centuries are earthenwares and stonewares manufactured by Josiah Wedgwood in England.[34] The monumental jasperware Wedgwood vase (fig. 22), with applied relief decoration depicting Apollo and the Muses, is almost identical to one illustrated in Wedgwood's 1787 trade catalogue (no. 266). Research over the past decade has revealed that in 1793 Philadelphia fancygoods merchant John Bringhurst (1722–1810) placed several orders with Wedgwood: one was for twelve vases, the most expensive of which cost £5.5.0 and had snake handles and reliefs of the Muses.

Wedgwood's vases, or imported English and French silver, may have inspired American silversmiths, such as Thomas Fletcher (1787–1866) and Sidney Gardiner (1785–1827), working in Philadelphia between 1811 and 1827. However, the covered ewer (fig. 23) that they fashioned during their work in Philadelphia seems to reflect French designs more strongly than English. The urn-shaped ewer was an exceedingly popular form during this period both abroad and in America. Like its ancient classical precedent, it was probably intended for use in the service of wine. Fletcher's travels to England and France in 1815 and 1825 not only resulted in his purchase of luxury items to sell at home, but also added greatly to his knowledge of what was fashionable and marketable at the time.[35]

Among the necessary luxuries for furnishing a tasteful interior in the first quarter of the nineteenth century would have been an elegant pair of candelabra to place on an impressive pier table, a pair of pedestals, a mantel, or down the center of a dining table. The most desirable candelabra were often those imported from France, and a number of these elaborately fashioned objects with American histories of original ownership survive.[36] Sometimes candelabra were placed on mantels, as Rosalie Stier Calvert of Maryland intended when she wrote her father in Antwerp in November 1806: "In my letter I asked you to please send me a pair of candelabra to place on the mantel in the drawing room in the same style as the ones you had here, with bronze figures (those are the nicest I have ever seen)." Presumably Rosalie's father was unable to fulfill her request, for a year later she wrote to him saying "I will have them sent from London....One of our best friends, Mr. Foster, who is presently embassy secretary, is returning to London. He is a man of taste and someone to whom I can explain exactly what I want as well as at what price."[37]

Although Winterthur's magnificent two pairs of similar ormolu (gilt brass) candelabra (fig. 24) do not have a history of original American ownership, ones similar to them could have been in America. In 1825, when purchasing items in Paris for resale in Philadelphia, Thomas Fletcher ordered "a pair of candelabra dorée [gilt]."[38] These rich and elegant candelabra are in the form of the three Graces, who personified grace and beauty. Each one holds up a torch capped with a basket of fruit; when the fruit is removed, the basket serves as a candle socket. The central flaming torch is also a candle socket, allowing each candelabrum to hold four lights. These candelabra were modeled after ones designed in 1810 by Parisian artist Pierre Paul Prud'hon for Napoleon's bride, the empress Marie-Louise. The royal candelabra were executed in silver and lapis lazuli by silversmith Jean-Baptiste Claude Odiot and brass worker Pierre-Philippe Thomire. Using Prud'hon's design, Thomire later made many copies in gilt brass like the Winterthur examples (fig. 24).

Stylish urban consumers of the day also patronized French emigré cabinetmaker Charles-Honoré Lannuier (1779–1819). Arriving in New York City in 1803 and initially living with his older brother Auguste (who had come to New York in the 1790s and established a prominent confectionary shop at 100 Broadway, a most fashionable address), Lannuier was soon producing extraordinary quality high-style furniture to meet the demands of his clients. Often copying French design sources that he may have brought with him or received from his Parisian cabinetmaker brother Nicolas, Lannuier also responded to the desires of clients who wanted furniture more closely derived from English styles, as seen in a pier table (fig. 25) that du Pont bought from Louis Guerineau Myers in 1930. This table was the first of eight pieces of furniture labeled or stamped by Lannuier that would eventually come into du Pont's collection, for even early in his collecting career, H.F. recognized the importance of objects that were marked by their maker. Thus, Winterthur is the richest institution in documented work by this important early nineteenth-century cabinetmaker.[39] Pier tables were typically made to be placed on the architectural "pier" between two windows, often with a large vertically proportioned looking glass or mirror hung over the table (see fig. 25). Though not labeled by its maker, this mirror represents some of the finest quality New York craftsmanship. Typical of those believed to be made either in Albany or New York City, the elaborately reverse-painted and gilt glass tablet across the top and the carved and gilt plinth with reverse-painted glass surmounting the top are regionally distinctive.

**24** | Candelabrum (one of a pair), Pierre-Philippe Thomire, Paris, 1810–1815 | Well-documented in elite American households is the presence of elegant imported candelabra that would have ornamented drawing rooms and provided shimmering illumination for evening parties.

**25** | Pier table, Charles-Honoré Lannuier, New York, 1805–1810; Looking glass, probably Albany, New York, 1790–1810; Candelabra, Pierre-Philippe Thomire, Paris, 1810–1815; Clock, Jean-Baptiste Dubuc, Paris, 1804–1817 | This rich ensemble of imported and American-made furnishings represents the elegant ambience in well-appointed American homes during the first quarter of the nineteenth century.

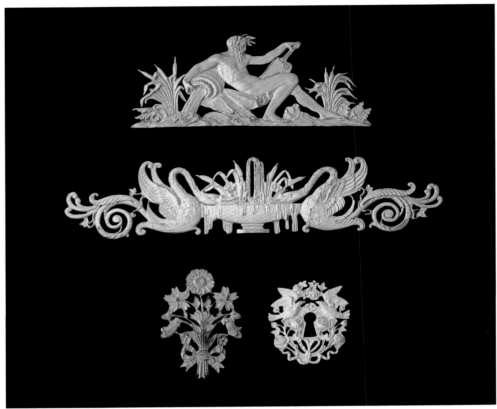

**26** | Illustration, from *Catalogue of Brass Knockers, Hinges, Escutcheons, Curtain Hooks, Bell Pulls and Rings, Night Bolts, Brass Ornaments, Curtain Rods, Etc.* (possibly Birmingham, England, 1822) | A wide variety of brass furniture hardware and ornamental mounts was available through local merchants, who had illustrated manufacturers catalogues from which to select the desired items.

**27** | Gilt brass mounts, France, 1810–1830 | Cast brass furniture mounts (finished to resemble gold by either mercury-gilding or coating with tinted lacquers) were imported into America to be used as "caps," "bases," or elaborate central ornaments on furniture produced in the late classical style.

Much of Lannuier's furniture, as well as that of other cabinetmakers working in New York and other urban centers, was decorated with ornamental metal mounts finished to resemble gold by either fire-gilding or coating with tinted lacquers. Lannuier may have obtained many of his very high quality mounts directly from a Parisian manufacturer, or perhaps through his brother Nicolas, who was working in Paris and who had presumably trained Honoré. However, most cabinetmakers ordered these rich ornaments, along with various other necessary brass fixtures like handles or fittings for roller blinds, from abroad through local hardware merchants who often had illustrated catalogues produced by the manufacturers (fig. 26).[40] These hardware catalogues represented just one type of trade catalogue merchants used to order a wide variety of goods from English and European manufacturers. Winterthur's library is especially rich in a wide variety of eighteenth- and early nineteenth-century publications of this type. In a few rare instances, hardware trade catalogues even contained actual samples.[41]

Mounts could be obtained in a variety of forms and ornaments for use on different types of furniture, ranging from "caps" and "bases" that would have been fitted to columns on pier tables or work tables (see fig. 28), to elaborate central ornaments for pier tables.

**28** | Work table, Charles-Honoré Lannuier, New York, 1817 | This work table, with columns, carved paw feet, and superior brass mounts, represents Lannuier's extraordinary talents as a craftsman and his ability to create stylish objects for his wealthy clients.

A group of mounts at Winterthur (fig. 27) represents a rare survival of the unused stock presumably of an early nineteenth-century Boston cabinetmaker, Henry Kellam Hancock (working 1816–1851).[42] Preserved in the possession of a Hancock descendant, many of these metal mounts and fittings were still wrapped in their original paper, marked on the exterior with a brief description of what type of piece was contained within.

Lannuier's exquisitely designed and superbly executed work table (fig. 28) exemplifies the best of late classical furniture. Incorporating basic elements indicative of this period, such as columns, carved paw feet originally painted to resemble antique bronze, lyres, and a Greek key motif of stamped brass, this finely proportioned table is veneered with highly figured mahogany that is "book-matched" on the front and rear. Intended as a table at which ladies might read or write, it is fitted on the inside with a fabric covered surface that raises and lowers by means of a ratchet device, and with compart-

ments to the sides for the storage of ink bottles and writing implements. Frequently these multipurpose tables were fitted with a compartment or "pouch" beneath the upper boxlike section for the storage of embroidery and sewing stuffs. The Winterthur table never had such a pouch—a design choice perhaps made by the patron. The attachment of brass casters under the paw feet allowed the user to easily move this work space about the room to capture the best light, whether it be daylight or artificial light. This particular work table is believed to have been made in 1817 for Maria Bayard, daughter of New York merchant William Bayard, at the time of her marriage to Duncan Pearsall Campbell.

In addition to furniture makers such as Lannuier who came seeking opportunity in the newly formed republic, emigré silversmiths also contributed to the body of American-made fashionable goods. With firsthand knowledge of objects made in European style centers, these craftsmen could offer their clients the latest and most fashionable designs often at a cheaper price than specially imported products. Two interesting men who were born abroad and formed a productive partnership from 1809 to 1812 were Simon Chaudron (1758–1846) and Anthony Rasch (c. 1778–c. 1859). Chaudron was born in France, trained as a watchmaker in Switzerland, and lived in Saint Domingue (Haiti) from 1784 until settling in Philadelphia in 1793. Rasch was born in Bavaria and trained as a silversmith presumably in Germany, though he may have worked in Paris or another major European style center prior to arriving in Philadelphia in 1804. Based on work he executed before his partnership with Chaudron, Rasch was not

**29** | Coffee and tea service, Anthony Rasch and Simon Chaudron, Philadelphia, 1809–1812 | When Chaudron and Rasch were in partnership, they created some of the most intriguing pieces of classically inspired silver. The range of classical ornament used on this five-piece coffee and tea service includes numerous animals, such as dogs, goats, and rams.

only a superior craftsman, but also a fully conversant practitioner of the highest style Parisian designs derived from those drawn by Charles Percier and Pierre F. L. Fontaine, Napoleon's architects and interior designers.[43]

Brief though it was, the Chaudron and Rasch partnership produced outstanding pieces of late classical silver distinguished in several ways. The stamp that they placed on their products reveals much about their relationship and salesmanship. Their mark is composed of two separate stamps, each a wavy banner shape; the first mark reads "CHAUDRON'S & RASCH," suggesting proprietorship on the part of Chaudron while also giving credit to Rasch; the second mark in a banner reads "STER · AMERI · MAN ·" for Sterling American Manufacture—this rare early use of the word "sterling" also patriotically suggests pride and smart salesmanship, as the new nation encouraged home manufactories. An unusual coffee and tea service (fig. 29) produced by this partnership references antiquity in both its forms and ornament. The incurved triangular base on all the pieces echoes ancient Roman tripod candelabra, and the overall shape of the covered sugar urn raised on curved supports with cloven feet is derived from forms known from archaeological digs and published design sources. The various animals seen as spouts, handles, terminals, and simply ornaments all can be found in antiquity, as can the garlands of grapes and grape leaves.

**30** | Sugar tongs, Maltby Pelletreau, John Bennett, and D.C. Cooke, New York, 1815–1828 | Although one of the smallest accoutrements used in the art of serving tea, these sugar tongs carry an ornament that evokes an important ancient culture, that of Egypt, reflected through the eyes of the early nineteenth century.

Sugar tongs were a necessary accessory in the service of tea and coffee, and although they were produced in some quantity in the first part of the nineteenth century, they were almost never made as part of a service. The pair (fig. 30) marked by John Bennett, Maltby Pelletreau, and D. C. Cooke of New York and Charleston, South Carolina, and dating from 1815 to 1828, are distinctive because they combine both Grecian and Egyptian references in the female figures (herms) carrying baskets of fruit upon their heads. Part Greek caryatid and part Egyptian queen, these implements of die-stamped manufacture suggested the exotic ancient past and served a very modern purpose in households of the late classical revival. Although references to the antiquities of ancient Egypt were limited in this period, they seen to have appeared most frequently in association with the functions of eating and drinking, in furniture forms such as cellarettes and sideboards, as well as on porcelain dinner services. One of the major illustrative sources for Egyptian forms and motifs in the period was a book sponsored by Napoleon and produced by his chief "art historian" Vivant Denon, who in 1798 accompanied Napoleon's forces to Egypt and under orders from him made detailed drawings of both ancient and modern Egypt. Between 1802 and 1829 Denon's drawings were published in ten monumental volumes as the *Description de l'Egypte,* a tome that was in private American libraries in the period.[44]

Privately sponsored academies and library associations were among the major repositories for contemporary source material relating to the ancient world in the early republic. The Library Company of Philadelphia was one of the earliest of these organizations, founded in 1731 by Benjamin Franklin and Thomas Cadwalader. By 1789 plans were being made for a new building on Fifth Street in Philadelphia. An enterprising young artist who had recently left the city to paint and study in London heard of this enterprise and approached the directors about executing a painting of an appropriate historic scene for the main room in the new edifice. Surprisingly, the directors liked young Samuel Jennings' idea and commissioned him to do a painting, though they had more specific direction for him concerning the subject. They requested an image of "Liberty (with her Cap and proper insignia) displaying the arts by some of the most striking Symbols of Painting, Architecture, Mechanics, Astronomy & ca., whilst She appears in the attitude of placing on the top of the Pedestal, a pile of Books, lettered with, *Agriculture, Commerce, Philosophy & Catalogue of Philadelphia Library*."[45] Since many directors were sympathetic to the antislavery movement, they also requested Jennings paint "A Broken Chain under her [Liberty's] feet, and in the distant back ground a Groupe of Negroes sitting on the Earth, or in some attitude expressive of Ease & Joy."[46] The resulting composition (fig. 31) was an incredibly compelling and prophetic portrayal heralding events that would change America in the next century. Jennings' original canvas still hangs in the Library Company of Philadelphia today, and Winterthur's version is one that the artist made so that the image might be engraved for public consumption and private profit. Unfortunately, this venture was never carried forward and the broader American public was deprived of the opportunity to review the sentiments of these enlightened directors.

The urban Philadelphia scene that the directors of the Library Company (and craftsmen like Fletcher and Gardiner, and Chaudron and Rasch) knew was not the idyllic fantasy that Jennings created for the private consumption of the members of the Library Company. More instructive for students of history is the work of John Lewis Krimmel (1786–1821), a German-trained emigré artist who arrived in America in 1810. His portrayals of both mundane domestic scenes and major public events have left a rich repository of images and expressions of people, places, and customs in early nineteenth-century America. Krimmel typically made numerous meticulous sketches prior to his final compositions. Among the great treasures of Winterthur's library are seven books filled with these descriptive sketches and studies. His 1815 oil on canvas, *Election Day in Philadelphia* (fig. 32), is not only a telling depiction of political unrest and conflict,

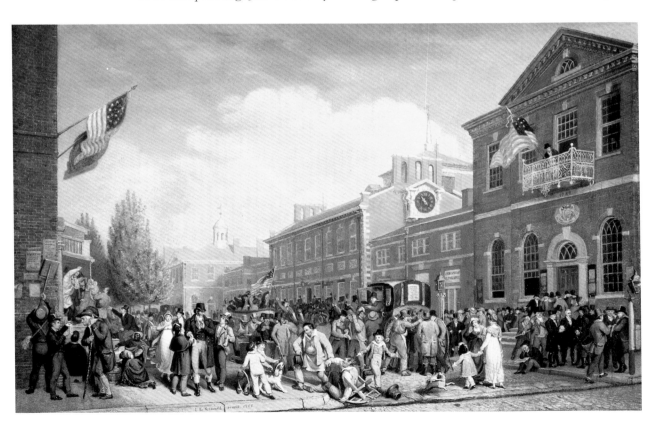

but also, in its smaller points, a brilliant encyclopedic rendering of costume, architecture, humanity, and societal customs. William Dunlap, the great early nineteenth-century biographer of America's artists, called Krimmel's *Election Day* "a great composition …executed with taste, truth, and feeling, both of pathos and humor, that rivals, in many respects, the best works of this description in either hemisphere."[47] Though the engraving of this image as an economic venture never came to fruition, it was one of the few pictures Krimmel executed as a commission intended for public consumption.

As the new nation (with great fervor and high hopes) moved forward in forming the essentials of government, emblems symbolic of this new nationality were emblazoned on a vast variety of both private and public objects. Henry Francis du Pont, despite his strong European heritage, did not miss a chance to acquire objects symbolizing national pride and patriotism. From engraved glass tablewares, silver skippets,[48] and bolder, more demonstrative expressions such as a monumental pier glass (see detail, page 150), Winterthur's collection abounds in patriotic memorabilia, enhancing the museum's representation of America's aesthetic and material heritage. Though the original situation of the grand "E Pluribus Unum" pier glass is unknown, it was most likely specially commissioned for a high-ceilinged room in either a public space or domestic setting. Towering a little over seven feet, this impressive looking glass, which has a history of ownership in the Rapelye and Totten families of Brooklyn, was most likely made in New York. Du Pont paired it with an unusual combination pier table and collector's cabinet (fig. 33) and placed the ensemble at the north end of his sixth-floor hallway, where they provided a stunning vista for guests.[49] Acquired in 1935 from the York, Pennsylvania, dealer Joe Kindig Jr., this totally unique eagle-supported collector's cabinet was certainly a special commission from a collector of natural specimens, such as shells or minerals (dilettante gentlemen in the first half of the nineteenth century often participated in this popular pastime). Related in its elaborate use of satinwood to several other exceptional Philadelphia pieces,[50] the richly veneered and rayed top lifts to reveal an interior space intricately divided into compartments for various sized specimens. Additionally, the inside of the top is fully mirrored to reflect the collection instantly as the top is raised even a small amount.

The Philadelphian who commissioned and housed a collection in this remarkable cabinet is not known, yet other collectors of the period certainly gathered and displayed natural wonders. For instance, the noted New York art aficionado Luman Reed (1785–1836) not only owned a great paintings collection, but also displayed in his picture gallery six cases containing specimens of shells and minerals collected from all over the world with the assistance of his son-in-law Theodore Allen.[51] Perhaps when du Pont first saw this cabinet he was reminded of his own initial acquisitions as a youth, roaming the fields and woodlands of Winterthur and collecting mineral specimens and bird eggs. Unquestionably a born collector, whether of trees, plants, pottery, fabrics, or furniture, Henry Francis du Pont, through his legacy, will for all time continue to inspire and enlighten those who encounter his wondrous American vision, Winterthur.

**33** | Collector's cabinet, Philadelphia, 1810–1820 | This unusual piece at first resembles a pier table, but the weighty top lifts to reveal intricately divided compartments for various sized specimens such as shells or minerals. Collecting such specimens was a popular pastime in the early nineteenth century.

190

## Notes

### Winterthur: An American Country Estate

**1.** This quote and additional biographical information are taken from Ruth Lord, *Henry F. du Pont and Winterthur: A Daughter's Portrait* (New Haven, 1999); Ruth Lord's description of entering Winterthur appears on page 130.

**2.** Du Pont was heavily influenced by the color and design theories of two turn-of-the-century British horticulturists: William Robinson, author of *The Wild Garden* (1870), and Gertrude Jekyll, author of *Wood and Garden* (1899).

**3.** Jacqueline Kennedy to Henry Francis du Pont, 8 May 1961, Winterthur Archives.

**4.** Elizabeth Stillinger, *The Antiquers* (New York, 1980), 222.

**5.** Lord 1999, 62.

**6.** Henry Francis du Pont's unpublished "Foreword," Winterthur Archives, written for Joseph Downs, *American Furniture, Queen Anne and Chippendale Periods* (New York, 1952). The pine dresser and its Staffordshire china are on permanent display at Winterthur as the gift of the Webb family.

**7.** Henry Francis du Pont, "Foreword," in Joseph Downs, *American Furniture, Queen Anne and Chippendale Periods*, rev. ed. (Atglen, Pa., 2001), v.

**8.** Unpublished "Foreword," Winterthur Archives.

**9.** Joshua Ruff and William Ayres, "H. F. du Pont's Chestertown House, Southhampton, New York," *The Magazine Antiques* 160, no. 1 (July 2001), 102.

**10.** Wendy A. Cooper, "H.F. du Pont's Fondness for Furniture: A Collecting Odyssey," *The Magazine Antiques* 161, no. 1 (January 2002), 158–163.

**11.** For a more complete history on the emerging popularity of American antiques see the chapter "The Collector in America" in Jay E. Cantor, *Winterthur* (New York, 1985, expanded and updated 1997), 89–104. For more on the important early collectors, see Stillinger 1980.

**12.** Thomas B. Parker to H. F. du Pont, 3 September 1926, Winterthur Archives; also quoted in Ruff and Ayres 2001, 99.

**13.** Unpublished "Foreword," Winterthur Archives.

**14.** H. F. du Pont to Henry Sleeper, 13 November 1930, Winterthur Museum registrar's office; also quoted in Stillinger 1980, 224.

**15.** Stillinger 1980, 228.

**16.** For more on this landmark exhibition, see Wendy A. Cooper, *In Praise of America; American Decorative Arts, 1650–1830* (New York, 1980), 4–13.

**17.** Louis Guerineau Myers to H. F. du Pont, 26 August 1929, Winterthur Archives; also quoted in Cooper 2002.

**18.** Henry Francis du Pont to Dr. Harlan Phillips, 25 March 1962, Winterthur Archives.

**19.** "The Reminiscences of Henry Francis du Pont," as quoted in Stillinger 1980, 225.

**20.** Cooper 1980, 4.

**21.** Cantor 1985, 159.

**22.** "The Meeting at Winterthur," Walpole Society *Note Book* (1932), 22.

**23.** "The Meeting at Winterthur" 1932, 26.

**24.** Elaine Rice Bachmann, "Jacqueline Kennedy, H. F. du Pont, and the Ultimate Historic House Restoration, *Winterthur Magazine* (Winter 2001), 43.

**25.** Bachmann 2001, 43, 45.

**26.** Cooper 2002.

**27.** Henry Francis du Pont, "A Possible Future: The Winterthur Museum," Willits Report, 1961, Winterthur Archives.

**28.** Henry Francis du Pont, instructions to "the executors of my will, to the officers of the Winterthur Corporation, and to the…Officers, and Director of the Henry Francis du Pont Winterthur Museum," c. 1964, Winterthur Archives.

### chapter 1
### Early Settlement and Sophistication

**1.** The first major exhibition in the past quarter century to explode this myth and add substantially to our knowledge of the period was *New England Begins: The Seventeenth Century* at the Museum of Fine Arts, Boston, in 1982.

**2.** For Peter Woodbury's will and inventory, see Essex County Probate Records, Docket #A-30481. For recent research on the Woodbury cupboard and a related group of case furniture, see Robert F. Trent, Peter Follansbee, and Alan Miller, "First Flowers of the Wilderness: Mannerist Furniture from a Northern Essex County, Massachusetts, Shop," in *American Furniture*, Chipstone Foundation Series (Milwaukee, 2001), 1–64.

**3.** Ronald William Fuchs II, "'A Venice Glass of Sack;' Elite Dining in Seventeenth-Century Virginia" (master's thesis, University of Delaware, 1996), 37.

**4.** Jean McClure Mudge, *Chinese Export Porcelain in North America* (New York, 1986), 93–95.

**5.** Fuchs 1996, 55.

**6.** Mudge 1986, 99.

**7.** Donald L. Fennimore, *Metalwork in Early America* (Winterthur, 1996), 33.

**8.** Abbott Lowell Cummings, *Rural Household Inventories 1675–1775* (Boston, 1964), 25 and 68.

**9.** Cummings 1964, xvi.

**10.** Less than five other American paintings from the first half of the eighteenth century survive to document this rare importation. For a greater discussion of early carpets in the colonies, see Sarah B. Sherrill, *Carpets and Rugs of Europe and America* (New York, 1996), 237–240.

**11.** According to a nineteenth-century handwritten note on the back of the painting, the portrait portrays Mrs. David Courter Marinus at nineteen years old. However, this portrait has been attributed to Gerret Duyckinck, who died one year after Mrs. Marinus was born; therefore, both the sitter and the artist are still in question.

**12.** James Hall, *Dictionary of Subjects and Symbols in Art* (London, 1974), 57.

**13.** Jonathan L. Fairbanks et al., *New England Begins: The Seventeenth Century,* vol. 3, [exh. cat., Museum of Fine Arts] (Boston, 1982), 497–499.

**14.** Boston 1982, 3:498.

**15.** Boston 1982, 3:485 and 494–495. Albert S. Roe, "Robert Sanderson's Silver Caudle Cup in the Winterthur Collection: The Turkey Motif in Seventeenth Century Design," *American Art Journal* 9, no. 1 (May 1977), 61–77.

**16.** Boston 1982, 3:482.

**17.** Boston 1982, 3:381.

**18.** Ian M. G. Quimby, *American Silver at Winterthur* (Winterthur, 1995), 194–195.

**19.** Deborah Dependahl Waters, ed., *Elegant Plate, Three Centuries of Precious Metals in New York City* (Hanover, N.H., and London, 2000), 172.

**20.** Benno M. Forman was the first to identify the Symonds in his 1968 University of Delaware master's thesis "The Seventeenth Century Case Furniture of Essex County, Massachusetts and Its Makers." Robert F. Trent continued that research in his essay "The Symonds Shops of Essex County, Massachusetts," in *The American Craftsman and the European Tradition* (Hanover, N.H., and London, 1989), 23–41.

**21.** For a recent survey of Symonds shop patrons and production, see Martha H. Willoughby, "Patronage in Early Salem: The Symonds Shops and Their Customers," in *American Furniture*, Chipstone Foundation Series (Milwaukee, 2000), 169–184.

**22.** Benno M. Forman, *American Seating Furniture 1630–1730* (London and New York, 1988), 85.

**23.** Cummings 1964, 46.

**24.** The other great chairs are owned by The Metropolitan Museum of Art, New York; The Museum of Fine Arts, Houston, The Bayou Bend Collection; Museum of Fine Arts, Boston; Pilgrim Hall Museum, Plymouth, Mass.; and Danvers Historical Society, Danvers, Mass.

**25.** This information was gleaned from the research notes of the late Benno M. Forman in the Winterthur Museum Archives. For recent research suggesting that Thomas Dennis was not the maker of the Staniford chest of drawers, see Trent, Follansbee, Miller 2001.

**26.** When John Staniford died in 1730, his widow Margaret moved in with her sister-in-law, Sarah Staniford, who had married John Heard. Later, when Margaret Staniford died, her possessions descended through the Heard family.

**27.** Another chest of drawers that bears some relationship to the Winterthur example has been attributed to the Symonds shop; it is owned by the Society for the Preservation of New England Antiquities and is illustrated in Trent 1989, 38.

**28.** Philip Zea, *The Great River* (Hartford, Conn., 1985), 204.

**29.** Philip Zea and Suzanne L. Flynt, *Hadley Chests* (Deerfield, Mass., 1992), 18–24.

**30.** For more on imported cane seating furniture, see Forman 1988, 229–267.

**31.** See Geoff Garbett and Ian Skelton, *The Wreck of the Metta Catharina* (Truro, 1987).

**32.** Robert G. Wheeler, "The Albany of Magdalena Douw," *Winterthur Portfolio* 4 (1968), 64–74.

**33.** Patricia Chapin O'Donnell, "Grisaille Decorated Kasten of New York," *The Magazine Antiques* 117, no. 5 (May 1980), 1108–1111.

**34.** Peter M. Kenny et al., *American Kasten* [exh. cat., The Metropolitan Museum of Art] (New York, 1991), 30.

**35.** New York 1991, 9.

**36.** New York 1991, 9.

**37.** Quimby 1995, 181–183 and 145–146.

**38.** In 1752 the colonies, like England, switched from the Julian (Old Style) Calendar—with the first day of the year being 25 March—to the Gregorian (New Style) Calendar—with the first day of the year being 1 January. Period documents indicate that Elizabeth Paddy Wensley died in February: when reckoned by the Julian Calendar she died in 1710, but with the shift of New Year's Day from 25 March back to 1 January, her year of death changed to 1711.

**39.** Boston 1982, 3:465.

**40.** Boston 1982, 3:436, 466–447.

## chapter 2
### East Meets West

**1.** Nancy E. Richards and Nancy Goyne Evans, *New England Furniture at Winterthur, Queen Anne and Chippendale Periods* (Winterthur, 1997), 311–313; and Morrison H. Heckscher, *American Furniture in The Metropolitan Museum of Art, II. Late Colonial Period, The Queen Anne and Chippendale Styles* (New York, 1985), 234–236.

**2.** Morrison H. Heckscher and Frances Gruber Safford, "Boston Japanned Furniture in the Metropolitan Museum of Art," *The Magazine Antiques* 129, no. 5 (May 1986), 1050. For information on a recently discovered French Huguenot emigré, Jean Berger, working as a painter-stainer in Boston, and presumably also as a japanner, from about 1718–1732, see Robert A. Leath, "Jean Berger's Design Book: Huguenot Tradesmen and the Dissemination of French Baroque Style," in *American Furniture*, Chipstone Foundation Series (Milwaukee, 1994), 136–161.

**3.** The three known high chests in this group are owned by Winterthur Museum (see Richards and Evans 1997, 307–310); The Museum of Fine Arts, Houston, The Bayou Bend Collection (see David B. Warren et al., *American Decorative Arts and Paintings in the Bayou Bend Collection* [Houston, 1998], 44–46); and The Metropolitan Museum of Art (see Heckscher 1985, 241–244). The Metropolitan's high chest has an accompanying dressing table with carved and gilt shell.

**4.** Heckscher and Safford 1986, 1051.

**5.** Richards and Evans 1997, 307–310.

**6.** Sinclair Hitchings, "Thomas Johnston," in *Boston Prints and Printmakers* (Charlottesville, Va., 1974), 87. Johnston attached this tradecard—proof of his work—to at least one tall clock, but the surface on that piece has been overpainted.

**7.** Dean A. Fales, "Boston Japanned Furniture," in *Boston Furniture of the Eighteenth Century* (Charlottesville, Va., 1974), 66–67.

8. Hitchings 1974, 126 – 128.

9. Heckscher and Safford 1986, 1053.

10. A japanned tall clock with decoration very similar to that on the Winterthur and the Henry Ford Museum examples is now owned by the Metropolitan Museum of Art (it was formerly owned by H. F. du Pont, then Winterthur Museum. See Heckscher and Safford 1986, 1060 – 1061).

11. The name Atkinson appears in white chalk inside the hood of the Winterthur tall clock; it may refer to James Atkinson, a clockmaker and watchmaker who emigrated from London in 1744 and settled in Boston, where he had a shop on Cornhill and later King Street, and died in 1756. Between 1752 and 1754 Gawen Brown also worked in King Street, therefore, it is possible that Brown may have acquired a case that Atkinson already had in stock. While it has been suggested that the Gawen Brown works are not original to this japanned case (see Alan Miller, "Roman Gusto in New England: An Eighteenth Century Boston Furniture Designer and His Shop," in *American Furniture*, Chipstone Foundation Series [Milwaukee, 1993], 184 – 185, 200), conclusive evidence does not at this time support this theory.

12. Warren 1998, 22 – 23; Sotheby's, *Highly Important Americana from the Stanley Paul Sax Collection* (New York, 16 – 17 January 1998), no. 441.

13. See Carl L. Crossman, *The Decorative Arts of the China Trade* (Antique Collectors' Club, Ltd., Suffolk, England, 1991), 266.

14. Linda Eaton, "Passage from India: Winterthur's Hand Painted Indian Export Cottons," *The Magazine Antiques* 161, no. 1 (January 2002), 172.

15. For more on Winterthur's collection of hand-painted Indian textiles, see Eaton 2002, 170 – 175.

16. Eaton 2002, 170.

17. Florence M. Montgomery, *Textiles in America 1650 – 1870* (New York, 1984), 314.

18. Eaton 2002, 172.

19. Eaton 2002, 172 – 173.

20. Montgomery 1984, 96.

21. Montgomery 1984, 96.

22. Montgomery 1984, 265.

23. Wendy A. Cooper, *In Praise of America: American Decorative Arts, 1650 – 1830* (New York, 1980), 53.

24. Gervase Jackson-Stops and James Pipkin, *The English Country House, A Grand Tour* (Boston, 1985), 175 – 179.

25. Crossman 1991, 306.

26. Margaret C. S. Christman, *Adventurous Pursuits, Americans and the China Trade, 1784 – 1844* (Washington, 1984) 68.

27. When objects such as fragile replicas of pagodas were shipped from China, they were attached to wooden bases and slid into obelisk-shaped packing boxes. A soapstone pagoda replica with its original packing box is at Historic Cherry Hill in Albany, New York; see David Sanctuary Howard, *New York and the China Trade* (New York, 1984), 129 – 130.

28. Josiah Quincy, *The Journals of Major Samuel Shaw, the First American Consul at Canton* (Boston, 1847), 196 - 197.

29. See *Views of the Pearl River Delta, Macao, Canton and Hong Kong* [exh. cat., The Peabody Essex Museum] (Salem, Mass., 1996), 124 - 125, no. 34.

30. May Brawley Hill, *Furnishing the Old-Fashioned Garden* (New York, 1998), 20.

31. William Chambers, *Designs of Chinese Buildings, Furniture, Dresses, Machines, and Utensils* (1757; reprint, New York, 1968), 1.

32. Donald L. Fennimore, *Metalwork in Early America, Copper and Its Alloys from the Winterthur Collection* (Winterthur, 1996), 131.

33. Nancy McClelland, *Historic Wallpapers* (Philadelphia, 1924), 100.

34. Crossman 1991, 403.

35. See Crossman 1991, 398 – 402, for a full discussion of these papers.

36. Crossman 1991, 391.

37. The other portion of the paper Davis installed in the home of E. Bruce Merriman in Providence, Rhode Island. The Merriman paper has subsequently been removed and is now owned by the Peabody Essex Museum in Salem, Massachusetts.

38. Joshua Ruff and William Ayres, "H. F. du Pont's Chestertown House, Southampton, New York," *The Magazine Antiques* 160, no. 1 (July 2001), 98 – 107.

39. Ruth Wales du Pont to her mother, 15 August 1930, RH Files, Winterthur Archives.

40. Crossman 1991, 401.

41. In recent years it has been ascertained that the three side chairs with pagoda crest-rails are actually of English origin, and they have had alterations to their legs.

42. H. F. du Pont's Letters to His Executors, 29 February 1964, Winterthur Archives, 65 – 66.

43. While this china table is the only Newport one of this form known, a closely related basin stand was recently dis-covered. With the same provenance as the china table (Bullock family), it has an identical pierced gallery and brackets. See *The Magazine Antiques* 156, 1 (July 1999), Advertisement of Israel Sack, Inc.

44. Richards and Evans 1997, 244.

45. Quincy 1847, 178 – 179.

46. Christman 1984, 148.

47. See Crossman 1991, 106 – 119, and 423 – 435, for an extensive discussion of these views.

48. See Jean McClure Mudge, *Chinese Export Porcelain in North America* (New York, 1986), 201.

49. The design of the border and four central floral motifs (exclusive of the eagle) is referred to as the FitzHugh pattern. This name presumably came from an English family (called FitzHugh) who were involved in the China trade in the eighteenth century and by the 1780s owned a set of porcelain of this design. While Chinese export porcelain in this pattern was produced in a variety of colors with different central motifs, blue was the most popular color. For more information on this specific pattern, see Jean McClure Mudge, *Chinese Export Porcelain for the American Trade* (Newark, Del., 1981), 163 – 166.

### chapter 3
### A Passion for Rococo

1. Joseph Downs, *American Furniture, Queen Anne and Chippendale* (New York, 1952), VI.

2. Joshua Ruff and William Ayres, "H. F. du Pont's Chestertown House, Southampton, New York," *The Magazine Antiques* 160, no. 1 (July 2001), 98 – 107.

**3.** American Art Association, Inc., *Colonial Furniture: The Superb Collection of the Late Howard Reifsnyder* (New York, 24 – 27 April 1929), lot no. 696, pages 260 – 261.

**4.** Downs 1952, VI.

**5.** Florence M. Montgomery, *Printed Textiles, English and American Cottons and Linens 1700 – 1850* (New York, 1970), 46.

**6.** *Eye for Excellence: Masterwork from Winterthur* [exh. cat., Winterthur Museum] (Winterthur, 1994), 56 – 57.

**7.** Graham Hood, *The Governor's Palace in Williamsburg* (Chapel Hill, N.C., 1991), 113, 128 – 129, 131 – 132, 287.

**8.** Jack L. Lindsey, *Worldly Goods, The Arts of Early Pennsylvania, 1680 – 1758* [exh. cat., Philadelphia Museum of Art] (Philadelphia, 1999), 28.

**9.** Over thirty years later, chimneybacks with the same royal arms motif were being produced in the colonies, such as the one made at Isaac Zane's Marlboro Furnace in Frederick County, Virginia, the form for which was carved by the London-trained carvers Nicholas Bernard and Martin Jugiez. See Wendy A. Cooper, *In Praise of America: American Decorative Arts, 1650 – 1830* (New York, 1980), 36 – 37.

**10.** Winterthur has a Webb chimneyback (acc. No. 56.101); for more on this, see Morrison H. Heckscher and Leslie Greene Bowman, *American Rococo* (New York, 1992), 220 – 221.

**11.** Heckscher and Bowman 1992, 220.

**12.** Betty Ring, *Girlhood Embroidery, American Samplers and Pictorial Needlework 1650 – 1850*, vol.1 (New York, 1993), 12 – 13.

**13.** Ring 1993, 1:44 – 53; see also Sotheby's *Important Americana* (Sale 6800, 19 – 21 January 1996), lot 1132.

**14.** Betty Ring has suggested that perhaps Suzanna Condy, a teacher and schoolmistress in Boston in the 1720s and 1730s began this "school of needlework," though she died just as it was reaching its peak. Ring further postulates that perhaps Condy's sister-in-law, Abigail Hillier, took over her students and continued her school.

**15.** For a fuller discussion of this table, see Nancy E. Richards and Nancy Goyne Evans, *New England Furniture at Winterthur, Queen Anne and Chippendale Periods* (Winterthur, 1997), 236 – 237.

**16.** For more on this house see Mabel Swan, "Two Early Massachusetts Houses," *The Magazine Antiques* 52, no.2 (August 1947), 107 – 109.

**17.** Dean Fales, *The Furniture of Historic Deerfield* (New York, 1996), 160; also Fairbanks et al., *Paul Revere's Boston* [exh. cat., Museum of Fine Arts] (Boston, 1975), 80 – 83.

**18.** Boston 1975, 44.

**19.** Robert Mussey and Anne Rogers Haley, "John Cogswell and Boston Bombé Furniture: Thirty-Five Years of Revolution in Politics and Design," in *American Furniture*, Chipstone Foundation Series (Milwaukee, 1994), 93. According to Morrison H. Heckscher (see his essay "English Furniture Pattern Books in Eighteenth-Century America" in the same volume, page 195), there were at least four editions of *Genteel Houshold Furniture*, each one enlarged. While Mussey cites the 1763 edition, the undated "II$^d$ Edition" in the Winterthur library appears to be the latest and largest with 350 designs in 120 copperplate engravings.

**20.** Mussey and Haley 1994, 98.

**21.** Mussey and Haley 1994, 98.

**22.** For a fuller discussion of these frames, see Morrison H. Heckscher, " Copley's Picture Frames," in Carrie Rebora, Paul Staiti, et al., *John Singleton Copley in America* [exh. cat., The Metropolitan Museum of Art] (New York, 1996), 143 – 161.

**23.** New York 1996, 130.

**24.** New York 1996, 170 – 172.

**25.** Heckscher and Bowman 1992, 6.

**26.** Graham Hood, *Bonnin and Morris of Philadelphia, The First American Porcelain Factory, 1770 – 1771* (Chapel Hill, N.H., 1972); Graham Hood, "The American China," in Francis J. Puig and Michael Conforti, eds., *The American Craftsman and the European Tradition* [exh. cat., The Minneapolis Institute of Arts] (Minneapolis, 1989), 240 – 255.

**27.** Donald L. Fennimore, *Metalwork in Early America, Copper and Its Alloys from the Winterthur Collection* (Winterthur, 1996), 232.

**28.** Heckscher and Bowman 1992, 214 – 217.

**29.** Jack L. Lindsey and Darrel Sewell, "The Cadwalader Family, Art and Style in Early Philadelphia," *Bulletin of the Philadelphia Museum of Art,* 91 (fall 1996), 21. For another looking glass (recently discovered) with a similar stone-colored surface treatment, see *Maine Antique Digest* (September 2001), 10-A. This glass was originally owned in the Barrell family and is now in the collection of the Society for the Preservation of New England Antiquities, Boston.

**30.** For a complete discussion of the Cadwaladers, their house, furniture, and portraits, see Lindsey and Sewell 1996, nos. 384 – 385.

**31.** All five of these paintings are owned by the Philadelphia Museum of Art today and are discussed in Lindsey and Sewell 1996, 24 – 34. The portraits were of John and Elizabeth Lloyd Cadwalader and their young daughter Anne, John's father, Dr. Thomas Cadwalader, his mother, Hannah Lambert Cadwalader, his unmarried brother, Lambert Cadwalader, and his sister, Martha Cadwalader Dagworthy.

**32.** Lillian B. Miller, ed., *The Peale Family, Creation of a legacy* (New York, 1996), 109 – 110.

**33.** Downs 1952, VI.

**34.** In addition to the carved frame looking glass (fig. 12) and the side chair (fig. 13), du Pont also acquired one of Cadwalader's four pole screens, a hairy paw foot card table, and four side chairs with hairy paw feet (different from fig. 13).

**35.** Charles F. Hummel, *A Winterthur Guide to American Chippendale Furniture, Mid-Atlantic and Southern Colonies* (Winterthur, 1976).

**36.** Judith Marla Guston, "The Almanacs of Michael Gratz: Time, Community, and Jewish Identity in Eighteenth-Century Philadelphia" (master's thesis, University of Delaware, 1999).

**37.** Guston 1999, 10

**38.** John D. Davis, *English Silver at Williamsburg* (Charlottesville, Va., 1976), 133–134.

**39.** The Lloyd family of Annapolis and Talbot County owned just such an oversized, London-made silver salver with engraved chinoiserie motifs surrounding the family coat of arms.

**40.** Morrison H. Heckscher, *American Furniture in The Metropolitan Museum of Art, II. Late Colonial Period, The Queen Anne and Chippendale Styles* (New York, 1985), 193.

**41.** Heckscher and Bowman 1992, 9.

**42.** Miller 1996, 126.

**43.** Edgar P. Richardson, *American Paintings and Related Pictures in the Henry Francis du Pont Museum* (Winterthur, 1986), 70.

**44.** Brandon Braeme Fortune with Deborah J. Warner, *Franklin and His Friends* [exh. cat., National Portrait Gallery] (Washington, 1999), 62.

**45.** Although the exact patrons who commissioned these side chairs are not known, the New York example is almost identical to a set originally owned by the Verplanck family (see Heckscher 1985, 75–77), and the Philadelphia example is closely related to ones owned in the Dickinson family.

**46.** New York 1996, 286–292.

**47.** New York 1996, 300.

**48.** Angela Mack et al., *Henry Benbridge, Charleston Portrait Painter (1743–1812)* [exh. cat., Gibbs Museum of Art] (Charleston, S.C., 2000), 6.

**49.** Elizabeth A. Fleming, "Staples for Genteel Living: The Importation of London Household Furnishings into Charleston During the 1780s," in *American Furniture*, Chipstone Foundation Series (Milwaukee, 1997), 335.

**50.** Mrs. Albert M. Wiggins Jr., Pittsburgh, Pa., to Winterthur registrar, 10 February 1970, letter and accompanying document from Mrs. Wiggins, "Brief Account of the Heath Family and Heathwood Hall, Columbia, S.C., Registrar's Office, Accession file 60.1071.

**51.** Wendy A. Cooper and Tara L. Gleason, "A Different Block and Shell Story: Providence Provenances and Pitch-Pediments," in *American Furniture*, Chipstone Foundation Series (Milwaukee, 1999), 162–208.

## chapter 4

## The Arts of the Pennsylvania Germans

**1.** Beatrice B. Garvan and Charles F. Hummel, *The Pennsylvania Germans, A Celebration of Their Arts, 1683–1850* [exh. cat., Philadelphia Museum of Art] (Philadelphia, 1982), 99.

**2.** Philadelphia 1982, 99.

**3.** Benjamin Rush, M.D., *An Account of the Manners of the German Inhabitants of Pennsylvania, 1789* (Philadelphia, 1789; reprint 1875), 5.

**4.** For an excellent discourse on H. F. du Pont's Pennsylvania German collecting adventures, see Scott T. Swank, "Henry Francis du Pont and Pennsylvania German Folk Art," in *Art of the Pennsylvania Germans* (New York and London, 1983), 77–101. It should also be noted that du Pont focused his collecting of Pennsylvania German material on the most visually arresting objects, which were often the most Germanic.

**5.** See Philadelphia 1982, 33, pl. 11.

**6.** The most frequently found documented or attributed chests are by Christian Seltzer (working in Jonestown, Bethel Township, Lebanon County) and Johannes and Peter Ranck, trained by Seltzer. For a recent study of the accounts of Peter Ranck, see Stephen Perkins, "Command You Me From Play Every Minute of the Day: Peter Rank, Jonestown Pennsylvania" (master's thesis, University of Delaware, 2001).

**7.** Winterthur owns a salt box (1958.17) and two tape looms (1965.2267 and 1959.2812) by Drissell. See "1997 Loan Exhibit — 'Pioneering Americana' — A Mercer Centennial," in *The 1997 Philadelphia Antiques Show* [The Philadelphia Antiques Show] (Philadelphia, 1997), 32–68; John and Martha S. Cummings, "John Drissell and His Boxes," Pennsylvania Folklife 9, no. 4 (fall 1958), 28–31; and Lita Solis-Cohen, "The Greater York Antiques Show," *Maine Antique Digest* (August 2001), 44c–47c (spoon cabinet ill. on 45c).

**8.** Heinrich B. Sage of Reading, Pennsylvania, produced a broadside in the early nineteenth century that is virtually identical to the painting on Winterthur's Adam and Eve chest (I thank Charles Hummel for this information).

**9.** For more on Strickler, see Donald R. Walters, "Jacob Strickler, Shenandoah County, Virginia, Fraktur Artist," *The Magazine Antiques* 110, no. 3 (September 1976), 536–543.

**10.** Donald Walters, "Johannes Spitler, Shenandoah County, Virginia, Furniture Decorator," *The Magazine Antiques* (October 1975), 730–735.

**11.** See John Bivins Jr.'s book (*The Moravian Potters in North Carolina* [Chapel Hill, N.C., 1972]) and his eponymous article focusing on the years 1756–1821 (*Ceramics in America*, Winterthur Conference Report 1972 [Winterthur, 1973]).

**12.** Frederick S. Weiser and Mary-Hammond Sullivan, "Decorated Furniture of the Schwaben Creek Valley," in *Ebbes fer Alle-Ebber, Ebbes fer Dich: Something for Everyone, Something for You*, Publications of the Pennsylvania German Society, vol. 14 (Breinigsville, Pa., 1980), 332–394. See also Benno M. Forman, "German Influences on Pennsylvania Furniture," in Swank 1983, 130–134.

**13.** Walters 1976, 541.

**14.** For more detail on the removal of this room to Winterthur, see Swank 1983, 84–95.

**15.** While this desk and bookcase has always been thought to be of Pennsylvania origin, it has recently been suggested that the piece may have been made in Shenandoah County, Virginia. Discussions with Sumpter T. Priddy III have raised this possibility, and future research may more assuredly confirm this theory.

16. American Art Association, Inc., *Colonial Furniture: The Superb Collection of the Late Howard Reifsnyder* (New York, 24–27 April 1929), lot no. 492, page 127.

17. Land surveys exhibiting Paul's fine calligraphy along with his surveying skills are occasionally seen today in the marketplace. Pook & Pook, Inc., *Important American Folk Art from the Private Collection of Mr. and Mrs. Paul Flack* (Downington, Pa., 28 October 2000), lot no. 36, page 6.

18. See Frank Sommer's essay in Swank 1983, 295.

19. For more on Schimmel, see Richard S. and Rosemarie B. Machmer, *Just for Nice, Carving and Whittling Magic of Southeastern Pennsylvania* (Reading, Pa., 1991), 74–75; for further information on the artist and the painted surfaces of five examples of his work in Winterthur's collection, see Danielle Snowflack, "Analytical Report No. 4261," September 2001, Winterthur Museum Analytical Laboratory.

20. Donald L. Fennimore, *Metalwork in Early America, Copper and Its Alloys from the Winterthur Collection* (Winterthur, 1996), 244–245, and Philadelphia 1982, 151, pl. 95.

21. Susan Burrows Swan, "Household Textiles," in Swank 1983, 224.

22. Oddly, spatterware seems to have been little used in its native England and was almost purely produced for export.

23. For a fuller essay on Winterthur's Pennsylvania German pottery, see Arlene Palmer Schwind, "Pennsylvania German Earthenware," in Swank 1983, 170–199.

24. Rush 1875, 60.

**chapter 5**

American Classicism

1. Graham Hood, "Early Neoclassicism in America," *The Magazine Antiques* 140, no. 6 (December 1991), 978–985.

2. Jonathan L. Fairbanks et al., *Paul Revere's Boston 1735–1818* [exh. cat., Museum of Fine Arts] (Boston, 1975), 186–187.

3. Wendy A. Cooper, *In Praise of America; American Decorative Arts, 1650–1830* (New York, 1980), 3.

4. Edgar P. Richardson, *American Paintings and Related Pictures in The Henry Francis du Pont Winterthur Museum* (Charlottesville, Va., 1986), 72.

5. For more on West and this painting, see Allan Staley et. al., *Benjamin West, American Painter at the English Court* [exh. cat., The Baltimore Museum of Art] (Baltimore, 1989), 57–59.

6. See Sumpter Priddy III, J. Michael Flanigan, and Gregory R. Weidman, "The Genesis of Neoclassic Style in Baltimore Furniture," in *American Furniture,* Chipston Foundation Series (Milwaukee, 2000), 59–99.

7. "Heart-back" is a period term that is found in price books produced in Philadelphia and New York in the 1790s and early 1800s. Chairs often called shield-back by collectors today were actually referred to in period price books as vase-back.

8. Robert Mussey of Boston, a furniture conservator and scholar, has been researching John and Thomas Seymour for the past decade, both in England and in America. In the fall of 2003 the Peabody Essex Museum in Salem, Massachusetts, plans to present a major exhibition (with an accompanying publication) that details the career of this important cabinetmaker, his contemporary environment, and his colleagues.

9. In *The Cabinet Dictionary* (London, 1803), Thomas Sheraton described the fabrication of the mechanism of tambour writing tables as "glued up in narrow slips of mahogany, and laid upon canvas which binds them together, and suffers them, at the same time, to yield to the motion their ends make in the curved groove in which they run, so that the top may be brought round to the front, and pushed at pleasure to the back again when it is required to be open." This description specifically refers to cylinder desks with tambour tops, but vertical tambours that roll back around the sides of the upper case are fabricated in the same manner.

10. *Exhibition and Sale at American Art Association–Anderson Galleries, Inc., Collection of Philip Flayderman* (New York, 2–4 January 1930), lot 451, pages 190–191. Although contemporary notations in Winterthur's Flayderman sale catalogue, as well as period newspaper reports, cite the price du Pont paid for this desk as $30,000, an invoice dated 12 April 1930 to du Pont from Collings and Collings bills H. F. $23,500 for "Antique Seymour & Son Desk, form [from] Flayderman." (This invoice is in Box HF 191, Collings and Collings Folder, Winterthur Archives.)

11. *Loan Exhibition of Eighteenth and Nineteenth Century Furniture and Glass for the Benefit of the National Council of Girl Scouts, Inc.* [exh. cat., The National Council of Girl Scouts, Inc.] (New York, 1929), no. 710.

12. See Paul S. Harris, "Gilbert Stuart and a Portrait of Mrs. Sarah Apthorp Morton," in *Winterthur Portfolio* 1 (1964), 198–220.

13. Florence M. Montgomery, *Printed Textiles, English and American Cottons and Linens 1700–1850* (New York, 1970), 281.

14. Susan Gray Detweiler (with Christine Meadows), *George Washington's China* (New York, 1982), 83.

15. Detweiler 1982, 86.

16. John Rhodehamel, *The Great Experiment, George Washington and the American Republic* (New Haven and London, 1999), 117.

17. Rhodehamel 1999, 122–124.

18. David B. Warren et al., *Marks of Achievement, Four Centuries of American Presentation Silver* (New York, 1987), 104–105.

19. Richardson 1986, 79.

20. Richardson 1986, 76.

21. Rhodehamel 1999, 155.

22. Rhodehamel 1999, 154.

23. Donald L. Fennimore, *Metalwork in America* (Winterthur, 1996), 303.

**24.** Joseph Downs, *American Furniture, Queen Anne and Chippendale Periods* (Winterthur, 1952), vi.

**25.** H. F. du Pont to Louis Guerineau Myers, 1 May 1931, box AD45, Winterthur Archives.

**26.** Montgomery 1970, 118 – 121. Whether or not this bill actually included the two armchairs that match the side chairs that were acquired is difficult to ascertain. Since the bill does not specify either "side" or "arm" chairs, it may be that the armchairs were just lumped together, or perhaps with every dozen chairs, two armchairs were included. The Bayard chairs and bill from Duncan Phyfe were inherited in 1912 by Bayard's granddaughter, Marie Louise Campbell. The bill from Phyfe totaled $1,434 and also included forty-two "Mahogany Chairs" at two different prices, three sofas, a sideboard, two pairs of card tables, a set of dining tables, a dressing table, a wardrobe, two tea tables, and a bason stand. Because Bayard also patronized the French emigré cabinetmaker Charles-Honoré Lannuier, who has recently been documented as the maker of chairs in this style, caution should always be exercised in associating documents with existing objects.

**27.** For a fuller discussion of period price books, see Benjamin A. Hewitt, Patricia E. Kane, Gerald W. R. Ward, *The Work of Many Hands: Card Tables in Federal America, 1790 – 1820* [exh. cat., Yale University Art Gallery] (New Haven, 1982).

**28.** Deborah D. Waters, "Is it Phyfe?" in *American Furniture*, Chipston Foundation Series (Milwaukee, 1996), 63 – 80.

**29.** Apparently Peale had complete control over the dress and posture of his sitters; in the case of the du Pont girls, they were rather critical of his directions and the results. See Lillian B. Miller with Carol Eaton Hevner and Ellen Hickey Grayson, *In Pursuit of Fame, Rembrandt Peale 1778 – 1860* [exh. cat., National Portrait Gallery] (Washington, 1992), 214 – 215.

**30.** Wendy A. Cooper, *Classical Taste in America 1800 – 1840* (New York, 1993), 105.

**31.** For a new perspective on painted suites of furniture, see Wendy A. Cooper, "American Painted Furniture: A New Perspective on Its Decoration and Use," *The Magazine Antiques* 161, no. 1 (January 2002), 212 – 217.

**32.** Sotheby's sale of the Collection of Andy Warhol, *Americana and European and American Paintings, Drawings, and Prints* (Sale 6000, vol. 5, 29 April 1988), lot 3184. This lot sold previously at Sotheby-Parke-Bernet, *Fine Americana* (Sale 4338, 30 January – 12 February 1980), lot 1628. A related pier table, not of the same set but probably from the same shop, is illustrated in *Baltimore Furniture: The Work of Baltimore and Annapolis Cabinetmakers from 1760 – 1810* [exh. cat., The Baltimore Museum of Art] (Baltimore, 1947), 158.

**33.** See Jack L. Lindsey, "An early Latrobe Furniture Commission," *The Magazine Antiques* 139, no. 1 (January 1991), 208 – 219.

**34.** Cooper 1993, 45; and Harwood A. Johnson and Diana Edwards, "Ornamental Wedgwood Wares in Philadelphia in 1793," *The Magazine Antiques* 145, no. 1 (January 1994), 166 – 173.

**35.** Donald L. Fennimore, "Thomas Fletcher and Sidney Gardiner: The Stylistic Development of Their Domestic Silver," *The Magazine Antiques* 102, no. 4 (October 1972), 644, fig. 3.

**36.** Cooper 1993, 39 – 40.

**37.** Margaret Law Callcott, ed., *Mistress of Riversdale: The Plantation Letters of Rosalie Stier Calvert 1795 – 1821* (Baltimore, 1991), 152 and 174.

**38.** Fennimore 1996, 225.

**39.** For an in-depth exploration of the life and career of Lannuier, see Peter M. Kenny, Frances F. Bretter, Ulrich Leber, *Honoré Lannuier, Cabinetmaker from Paris: The Life and Work of a French Ebeniste in Federal New York* [exh. cat., The Metropolitan Museum of Art] (New York, 1998).

**40.** Donald L. Fennimore, "Brass Hardware on American Furniture, Part II," Antiques 140 (July 1991), 80 – 91; and Jillian Ehninger, "Furniture Hardware from the Boston Workshop of Henry K. Hancock," *The Magazine Antiques* 147, no. 5 (May 1995), 732 – 739.

**41.** Cooper 1993, 184 – 185.

**42.** Cooper 1993, 184 – 186.

**43.** Cooper 1993, 146 – 147.

**44.** Cooper 1993, 66.

**45.** Richardson 1986, 84.

**46.** Richardson 1986, 84.

**47.** Anneliese E. Harding, *John Lewis Krimmel, Genre Artist of the Early Republic* (Winterthur, 1994), 83.

**48.** For glass at Winterthur engraved with the great seal, see Arlene Palmer, *Glass in Early America, Selections from the Henry Francis du Pont Winterthur Museum* (Winterthur, 1993), 75 – 77. For silver skippets, see Ian M. G. Quimby, *American Silver at Winterthur* (Winterthur, 1995), 397 – 398.

**49.** John A. H. Sweeney, *Winterthur Illustrated* (Winterthur, 1963), 130.

**50.** J. Michael Flanigan, *American Furniture from the Kaufman Collection* [exh. cat., National Gallery of Art] (Washington, 1986); and Charles F. Montgomery, *American Furniture, The Federal Period in the Henry Francis du Pont Winterthur Museum* (Winterthur, 1966), 420 – 422.

**51.** Ella M. Foshay, *Mr. Luman Reed's Picture Gallery* (New York, 1990), 39.

## List of Illustrated Objects

*Not all woods listed have been confirmed by microanalysis.*

*All dimensions are overall and cited in inches, with height preceding width preceding depth.*

### Winterthur: An American Country Estate

**Page 15**
*Henry Francis du Pont*, 1914
Ellen Emmet Rand (1876 – 1941),
New York
oil on canvas
55 ¼ × 31 ½
Bequest of Henry Francis
du Pont 1959.2623

**Page 18**
High chest, 1760 – 1780
Philadelphia
mahogany, tulip, red oak,
yellow pine, white cedar; brass
90 ¼ × 45 ⅝ × 25 ½
Gift of Henry Francis du Pont
1958.0592

**Page 23**
Dressing table, 1700 – 1720
Boston
black walnut, black walnut
veneer, maple, white pine;
slate; brass
25 ³⁄₁₆ × 29 ¾ × 22 ¹⁄₁₆
Museum purchase and
partial gift of Gregory M. Cook
1998.0001

### chapter 1
### Early Settlement and Sophistication

**Pages 26 (detail), 32**
Sugar box, 1702
Edward Winslow (1669 – 1753),
Boston
silver
5 × 7 ⁷⁄₁₆ × 6 ⅛
Gift of Henry Francis du Pont
1959.3363

**Page 28**
*Differents Pourtraicts de
Menuiserie* (Antwerp, 1588)
Hans Vredeman de Vries
7 ⅛ × 9 ¹³⁄₁₆
Courtesy, The Winterthur Library,
Printed Book and Periodical
Collection

**Page 29**
Cupboard, 1680
Possibly made by the Emery
Shop, probably Newbury,
Massachusetts
oak, sycamore, maple, black
walnut, tulip
57 ¾ × 50 × 21 ⅝
Bequest of Henry Francis
du Pont 1966.1261

Armchair, 1675 – 1700
New England
ash, hickory, elm
46 ⅞ × 23 ⅜ × 22 ¼
Gift of Henry Francis du Pont
1958.0680

Bowl, 1600 – 1625
Jingdezhen, China
porcelain
6 ⁹⁄₁₆; diam: 14 ¹³⁄₁₆
Gift of Osborne and Mary M.
Soverel 1992.0034

Plates, 1670 – 1710
Edmund Dolbeare (w. 1670 – 1711)
pewter
1 ⅜; diam: 15 ⅜
Gift of Henry Francis du Pont
1955.0060.001
Gift of Charles K. Davis
1955.0060.002

**Pages 29, 38 (top)**
Valuables cabinet, 1676
Attributed to the Symonds
Shop, Salem, Massachusetts
red oak, white oak, black
walnut, soft maple, white
pine; brass
17 ¼ × 17 × 9 ⅞
Gift of Henry Francis du Pont
1958.0526

**Pages 29, 30**
Plate, about 1643
Jingdezhen, China
porcelain
diam: 11 ½
Gift of Leo A. and Doris C.
Hodroff 2000.0061.002

**Pages 29, 36**
Tankard, about 1710
Jacob Boelen (1654 – 1729),
New York
silver
7; diam: 5 ⅜
Gift of Charles K. Davis
1957.0094

Tankard, about 1690
John Coney (1655 / 1656 – 1722),
Boston
silver
7 ⅛ × 8 ¼ × 5 ¹¹⁄₁₆
Museum purchase
1965.0033

**Pages 29, 31**
Candlesticks, 1650 – 1690
Nuremberg, Germany
brass
8; diam: 6 ¼
Bequest of Henry Francis
du Pont 1964.0693 – .0694

**Page 30**
Bowl, 1668
Probably Holland
tin-glazed earthenware
(delftware)
5 ⅛; diam: 9 ⅝
Bequest of Henry Francis
du Pont 1964.0535

**Page 32**
*Unknown Woman*, 1690 – 1700
Attributed to Gerret Duyckinck
(1660 – about 1710), New York
oil on panel
31 ½ × 24 ¼
Bequest of Henry Francis
du Pont 1956.0565

**Page 34**
Caudle cup, about 1675
Robert Sanderson (1608 – 1693),
Boston
silver
5 × 7 ¾; diam: 5 ¾
Gift of Henry Francis du Pont
1961.0504

Covered cup, about 1690
Jurian Blanck Jr. (c. 1645 –
1699 or 1714), New York
silver
5 ⅝ × 9; diam: 5 ⅝
Gift of Henry Francis du Pont
1959.2298

**Page 35**
Two-handled bowl, about 1735
Jacob Ten Eyck (1705 – 1793),
New York
silver
5 × 10 ⅞; diam: 7 ⁷⁄₁₆
Gift of Charles K. Davis 1955.0127

**Page 38 (bottom)**
Valuables cabinet, 1679
Attributed to the Symonds Shop,
Salem, Massachusetts
red oak, red cedar, black walnut,
soft maple; brass
16 ¾ × 17 ¼ × 9
Gift of Henry Francis du Pont
1957.0540

**Page 39**
Armchair, 1640 – 1685
Essex County, Massachusetts
red oak, white oak
36 ½ × 22 ¼ × 21
Gift of Henry Francis du Pont
1954.0073

Turned chair, 1650 – 1675
Boston
maple, ash, poplar
46 × 24 × 18
Gift of Henry Francis du Pont
1958.0681

**Page 40**
Chest of drawers, 1678
Attributed to Thomas Dennis
(1638 – 1706), Essex County,
Massachusetts
oak, maple, black walnut
42 × 44 ¾ × 19 ⅞
Gift of Henry Francis du Pont
1957.0541

**Page 41**
Chest of drawers, 1710 – 1720
Hadley, Massachusetts
red oak, white oak, yellow
pine, chestnut
45 ¼ × 43 ½ × 20 ¾
Museum purchase
1957.0054

**Page 45**
Armchair, 1695 – 1710
Boston
maple, red oak
53 1/4 × 24 × 27 1/2
Gift of Henry Francis du Pont
1958.0553

Armchair, 1690 – 1720
Philadelphia
black walnut
43 5/8 × 25 3/8 × 22 3/4
Gift of David Stockwell
1955.0130

**Page 46**
Dressing table, 1700 – 1725
Boston
black walnut, burl walnut
veneer, white pine, maple;
brass
30 3/4 × 33 3/4 × 21 1/2
Bequest of Henry Francis
du Pont 1958.0584

**Page 47**
*Magdalena Douw (Mrs. Harme
Gansevoort),* about 1740
Artist unknown (Hudson River
Valley, New York)
oil on canvas
51 1/16 × 33
Gift of Henry Francis du Pont
1963.0852

**Page 48**
*Officina Archularia*
(Amsterdam, 1642)
Crispijn van de Passe (d. 1670)
14 1/2 × 9 3/8
Courtesy, The Winterthur Library,
Printed Book and Periodical
Collection

**Page 49**
*Kast,* 1700 – 1735
New York
poplar, maple, painted
decoration
69 7/8 × 62 1/4 × 22 5/8
Bequest of Henry Francis
du Pont 1958.1144

Vases, 1670 – 1700
Netherlands
tin-glazed earthenware
13 5/8 × 6 7/8
Bequest of Henry Francis
du Pont 1961.1461.001 – .002

Jar and cover, 1670 – 1730
Netherlands
tin-glazed earthenware
16 7/8 × 9 1/8
Bequest of Henry Francis
du Pont 1961.1463a – b

**Page 50**
Chargers, 1711
Edward Winslow (1669 – 1753),
Boston
silver
2; diam: 15
Bequest of Henry Francis
du Pont 1966.1053 – .1054

**Pages 50, 51 (detail)**
Flagon, 1711
Peter Oliver (1682 – 1712), Boston
silver
12; diam: 6 3/8
Bequest of Henry Francis
du Pont 1966.1052

**chapter 2**
# East Meets West

**Pages 52 (detail), 54 – 55**
High chest, 1740 – 1750
John Pimm (d. 1773), Boston
black walnut, soft maple,
white pine; japanned dec-
oration; brass
95 3/4 × 42 × 24 1/2
Gift of Henry Francis du Pont
1957.1084

**Page 56**
*A Treatise of Japaning and
Varnishing* (Oxford, 1688)
John Stalker and George Parker
printed for and sold by the
authors
14 5/8 × 9 1/16
Courtesy, The Winterthur Library,
Printed Book and Periodical
Collection

**Page 59**
Tall clock, 1749 – 1755
Works by Gawen Brown (1719 –
1801), japanning attributed to
Thomas Johnston (1708 – 1767),
Boston
white pine; japanned
decoration; brass
94 1/2 × 22 1/4 × 10 3/4
Museum purchase
1955.0096.003

Side chair, 1735 – 1750
Boston
black walnut; japanned
decoration
39 3/4 × 21 1/4 × 17 3/4
Gift of Catherine C. Lastavica in
honor of E. McSherry Fowble
2000.0050.001

**Page 60**
Palampore, 1690 – 1720
India
hand-painted cotton
106 3/4 × 148 1/2
Gift of Henry Francis du Pont
1957.1290

**Page 61**
Needlework picture, 1754
Mary King, Philadelphia
silk and metallic yarns and
glass beads embroidered in
satin on silk moire
18 1/4 × 24 1/8
Bequest of Henry Francis
du Pont 1966.0978

**Page 63**
Quilt, 1795 – 1825
Eastern United States
cotton
100 × 92
Museum purchase with funds
provided by Mr. Samuel Pettit in
memory of his wife, Sally Pettit
2001.0021

**Page 64**
Plate-printed cotton,
1765 – 1775
England
cotton
112 × 36
Museum purchase
1958.0112.006d

Plate-printed cotton,
about 1785
England
cotton
53 × 12 1/2
Gift of Henry Francis du Pont
1955.0634.006

**Page 66**
*An Embassy from the East-
India Company of the United
Provinces, to the Grand Tartar
Cham Emperour of China*
(London, 1669)
John Nieuhoff (1618 – 1672)
printed by John Macock
for the author
16 1/16 × 10 3/8
Courtesy, The Winterthur Library,
Printed Book and Periodical
Collection

**Page 67**
Pagoda, 1785 – 1830
China
porcelain, gilt wooden finials
(possibly later replacements)
60 × 14 1/4
Bequest of Henry Francis
du Pont 1959.3381

**Page 68**
Andirons, 1760 – 1780
Probably England, possibly
Philadelphia
iron, brass
28 3/8 × 12 1/2 × 25
Gift of Henry Francis du Pont
1954.0092.001 – .002

Page 69
*Catalogue of Escutcheons,*
*Hinges, Drawer Pulls, Tea-chest*
*Handles, Candlesticks, Etcetera,*
(probably Birmingham,
England, about 1770)
7 ½ × 10 ½
Courtesy, The Winterthur Library,
Printed Book and Periodical
Collection

Pages 70 – 71 (far right), 73
China table, 1785 – 1800
Attributed to John Townsend
(1733 – 1809), Newport,
Rhode Island
mahogany, chestnut, white
pine, soft maple
27 ¼ × 34 ¼ × 21
Museum purchase
1958.0037

Page 73
Looking glass, 1760 – 1780
England
white pine, silvered glass
29 ¼ × 47
Museum purchase
1962.0070

Tea wares, 1786 – 1795
China
porcelain, gilt
5 ¾
Bequest of Henry Francis
du Pont 1963.0714

Page 74
*Digging the Ground for*
*Porcelain,* from Book of Chinese
Watercolors, 1800 – 1810
China
watercolor on paper
9 ⁷⁄₁₆ × 10
Museum purchase
1956.0038.106

*Loading Boats for Canton,*
from Book of Chinese Watercolors, 1800 – 1810
China
watercolor on paper
9 ⁷⁄₁₆ × 10
Museum purchase
1956.0038.127

Page 75 (left)
Punch bowl, 1735 – 1755
England
tin-glazed earthenware
(delftware)
5 ¼; diam: 12
Gift of Henry Francis du Pont
1958.0095.003

(right)
Bowl, 1710 – 1740
Jingdezhen, China
porcelain
2 ⁷⁄₁₆ ; diam: 4 ½
Museum purchase with special
funds for Collection Objects
provided by the Claneil Foundation 1976.0065

Page 76
Plate with the Vaughan
family coat of arms impaling
Hallowell, about 1755
Jingdezhen, China
porcelain
⁷⁄₈; diam: 8 ¹¹⁄₁₆
Gift of Wunsch Americana
Foundation 1976.0082.001

Bookplate of the Vaughan
family coat of arms impaling
Hallowell, 1747 – 1755
Probably England
paper
3 ¹⁵⁄₁₆ × 3 ³⁄₁₆
Courtesy, The Winterthur Library,
Joseph Downs Collection
of Manuscripts and Printed
Ephemera

Page 78
Hong punch bowl, 1788 – 1810
China
porcelain
5 ⁷⁄₈; diam: 14 ³⁄₈
Bequest of Henry Francis
du Pont 1961.1427

Page 79
*View of the Foreign Factories*
*in Canton,* 1800 – 1810
China
oil on canvas
28 ¼ × 40
Gift of Henry Francis du Pont
1965.1601

Pages 80 , 81 (detail)
Plate, 1800 – 1820
Jingdezhen, China
porcelain
⁷⁄₈; diam: 9 ¾
Bequest of Henry Francis
du Pont 1956.0548.011

## chapter 3
A Passion for Rococo

Page 86
Plate-printed cotton, 1765 – 1775
Nixon & Company, Phipps-
bridge, Surrey, England
cotton
104 ½ × 36
Bequest of Henry Francis
du Pont 1969.3889.003

Block-printed cotton, 1775 – 1790
England
cotton
60 ½ × 68
Museum purchase
1958.0073.001

Page 88
"The Four Continents,"
1760 – 1770
Derby Porcelain Factory,
Derbyshire, England
porcelain
12
Bequest of Henry Francis
du Pont 1958.2622.001 – .004

Page 89
Chimneyback, 1747
Oxford Furnace, Warren County,
New Jersey
iron
32 ¼ × 29 ¼
Bequest of Henry Francis
du Pont 1959.2531

Chimneyback, 1770 – 1774
Aetna Furnace (1766 – 1774),
Burlington County, New Jersey
iron
31 ½ × 30 × 1 ¹⁄₁₆
Bequest of Henry Francis
du Pont 1958.2750

Page 91
Needlework picture, 1748
Sarah Warren (d. 1797), Boston
silk, wool, linen; original
veneered and gilt frame;
brass sconce plates
25 ³⁄₈ × 52 ¼
Gift of Henry Francis du Pont
1962.0069

Page 92
Tea table, 1755 – 1765
Boston
mahogany, white pine
27 ½ × 30 ½ × 19 ³⁄₈
Bequest of Henry Francis
du Pont 1958.2774

Assembled tea set, 1730 – 1770
China
porcelain
5 ³⁄₁₆
Museum purchase
1959.0077.001 – .024, 1979.0114

Candlesticks, about 1720
John Burt (1692 – 1745), Boston
silver
7 ³⁄₁₆; diam: 4 ³⁄₈
Bequest of Henry Francis
du Pont 1967.1443.001 – .002

Page 94
Desk and bookcase, 1780 – 1795
Boston
mahogany, white pine,
yellow pine; brass; silvered glass
92 × 38 ³⁄₇ × 19 ¾
Gift of Henry Francis du Pont
1957.1396

Page 95
Plate 51, from *The 11ᵉ Edition*
*of Genteel Houshold Furniture*
*In the Present Taste* (London,
1764 or 1765)
Society of Upholsterers,
Cabinetmakers, etc.
printed by R. Sayer
9 ¹⁄₁₆ × 5 ¾
Courtesy, The Winterthur Library,
Printed Book and Periodical
Collection

*The Gore Children,* about 1755
John Singleton Copley
(1738 – 1815), Boston
oil on canvas
41 × 56 ½
Gift of Henry Francis du Pont
1959.3408

Pages 96, 97
Sconces, 1760 – 1780
London or Birmingham, England
brass
13 ½ × 11 × 9 ⅜
Museum purchase
1957.0126.026 – .027

Page 97
Card table, 1765 – 1780
Philadelphia
mahogany, oak, cedar
27 ⅜ × 34 × 32 ¾
Gift of Henry Francis du Pont
1960.1059

Grand Platt Menage, 1775 – 1810
Staffordshire or Yorkshire,
England
cream-colored earthenware
(creamware)
29 ¼; diam: 14 ¼
Museum purchase with funds
provided by Collector's Circle
2000.0005

Looking glass, 1770 – 1771
Attributed to James Reynolds
(1736 – 1794), Philadelphia
pine, tulip; silvered glass
55 ½ × 28 ¼ × 3
Gift of Henry Francis du Pont
1952.0261

Page 99
Side chair, 1770
Attributed to shop of Thomas
Affleck (1740 – 1795), Philadelphia
mahogany, white cedar,
arbor vitae
36 ⅞ × 23 ½
Gift of Henry Francis du Pont
1958.2290

Page 100
Plate 16, from *The Gentleman
and Cabinet-Maker's Director*
(London, 1754)
Thomas Chippendale (1718 – 1779)
printed by J. Haberkorn
17 ½ × 11 ½
Courtesy, The Winterthur Library,
Printed Book and Periodical
Collection

Page 101
*The Edward Lloyd Family,* 1771
Charles Willson Peale
(1741 – 1827), Maryland
oil on canvas
48 × 57 ½
Museum purchase
1964.0124

Pages 102 – 103, 105
High chest, 1760 – 1770
Philadelphia
mahogany, white pine, tulip,
cedar; brass
102 ½ × 46 ⅛ × 24 ⅝
Gift of Henry Francis du Pont
1957.0506

Page 106
Dressing table, 1760 – 1770
Philadelphia
mahogany, yellow pine, tulip,
cedar; brass
28 ½ × 37 × 18 ¾
Gift of Henry Francis du Pont
1957.0505

Side chair, 1760 – 1770
Philadelphia
mahogany, yellow pine
40 × 24 ½ × 22
Museum purchase with funds
provided by Collector's Circle
1997.0034

Page 107
Salver, about 1750
Thomas Edwards (1701/1702 –
1755), Boston
silver
1 ¹⁵⁄₁₆; diam: 11 ⁷⁄₁₆
Gift of Henry Francis du Pont
1961.0938

Page 108
Tea table, 1765 – 1780
Philadelphia
mahogany
28 ⅛; diam: 34 ⅜
Gift of Henry Francis du Pont
1960.1061

Page 110
*Mrs. Benjamin Rush,* 1776
Charles Willson Peale
(1741 – 1827), Philadelphia
oil on canvas
49 × 39 ⅛
Gift of Mrs. T. Charlton Henry
1960.0392

*Benjamin Rush,* 1783 – 1786
Charles Willson Peale
(1741 – 1827), Philadelphia
oil on canvas
50 ¼ × 40
Gift of Mrs. T. Charlton Henry
1959.0160

Page 111 (left)
Side chair, 1760 – 1775
Philadelphia
mahogany, white pine,
white cedar
37 ¾ × 23 ½ × 22 ¾
Gift of Henry Francis du Pont
1952.0240.003

(right)
Side chair, 1760 – 1780
New York
mahogany, birch, soft maple
37 ⅞ × 24 ¼ × 22 ¾
Gift of Henry Francis du Pont
1952.0243

Page 112
*Mrs. Roger Morris,* 1771
John Singleton Copley
(1738 – 1815), New York
oil on canvas
30 × 24 ½
Museum purchase with funds
provided by Henry Francis du
Pont 1964.0023

Page 113
*John Purves and His Wife Eliza
Anne Pritchard,* 1775 – 1777
Henry Benbridge (1743 – 1812),
Charleston, South Carolina
oil on canvas
39 ½ × 50
Bequest of Henry Francis
du Pont 1960.0582

Page 114
Slab-top side table, 1760 – 1775
Possibly South Carolina or
Philadelphia
mahogany, yellow pine; marble
35 × 48 × 25
Bequest of Henry Francis
du Pont 1960.1071

Sweetmeat pole and baskets,
1760 – 1780
England
lead glass
17 ⅛; diam: 7 ⅛
Museum purchase
1979.0063a – r

Salver, 1760 – 1785
England
lead glass
6 ⅜; diam: 15 ⁹⁄₁₆
Museum purchase
1990.0086.001

Jelly glasses, 1760 – 1785
England
lead glass
3 ¾; diam: 2 ¼
Museum purchase
1990.0086.003 – .012

Pages 116, 117 (detail)
Chest on chest, 1775 – 1790
Providence, Rhode Island
mahogany, chestnut, white
pine; brass
96 × 40 × 22 ½
Bequest of Henry Francis
du Pont 1957.1394

### chapter 4
## The Arts of the Pennsylvania Germans

**Page 120**
Box, 1770–1800
Berks or Northampton County, Pennsylvania
white pine; paint; iron
9 3/16 × 15 11/16 × 8 1/2
Bequest of Henry Francis
du Pont 1959.2805

**Page 121**
Chest, 1765–1810
Berks County, Pennsylvania
white pine; paint; iron
27 3/4 × 51 × 22 3/4
Museum purchase
1955.0095.001

**Page 123**
Fraktur, about 1798
Possibly Mahantango Valley, Pennsylvania
watercolor on paper
12 7/8 × 16 3/4
Bequest of Henry Francis
du Pont 1961.1109

**Page 125**
Fraktur, 1794
Jacob Strickler (1770–1842), Page County, Virginia
watercolor on paper
12 1/8 × 15 1/8
Bequest of Henry Francis
du Pont 1957.1208

Lion, 1840–1865
John Bell Sr. (1800–1880), Waynesboro, Pennsylvania
lead-glazed earthenware
7 3/8 × 8 1/2
Bequest of Henry Francis
du Pont 1967.1630

**Page 126**
Desk, 1834
Schwaben Creek Valley, North-umberland County, Pennsylvania
tulip; paint; brass
49 1/8 × 39 × 19 3/4
Bequest of Henry Francis
du Pont 1964.1518

**Page 128**
*Shrank*, 1768
Lancaster County, Pennsylvania
black walnut, sulfur inlay; iron, brass
89 1/2 × 85 3/4 × 30 5/8
Bequest of Henry Francis
du Pont 1965.2262

**Pages 129, 134–135**
Candlesticks (two of a set of four), 1752–1781
Made and marked by Johann Christoph Heyne (1715–1781), Lancaster, Pennsylvania
pewter, tinned sheet iron
21 7/8 × 7 3/4 × 8 5/8
Gift of Henry Francis du Pont
1965.1602.001–.002

**Pages 130 (left), 134–135**
Slat-back side chair, 1725–1750
Delaware Valley, Pennsylvania
maple; rush seat
45 1/4 × 19 1/8 × 16 1/4
Bequest of Henry Francis
du Pont 1959.2332

**Page 130 (right)**
Slat-back side chair, 1725–1750
Delaware Valley, Pennsylvania
maple; black paint; rush seat
46 3/8 × 20 3/4 × 17 7/8
Bequest of Henry Francis
du Pont 1959.2402

**Page 131 (left)**
Armchair, 1770–1800
Bethlehem, Pennsylvania
black walnut; leather
48 × 23 × 21
Gift of H. Rodney Sharp
1958.3233

**(right)**
Armchair, 1753–1773
Lancaster, Pennsylvania
black walnut, pine; leather
47 × 22 1/8 × 18 1/4
Museum purchase
1958.0065

**Page 133**
Milk pan, 1797
John Strawn, Bucks County, Pennsylvania
earthenware
2 5/8; diam: 14 5/16
Bequest of Henry Francis
du Pont 1965.2302

**Pages 136, 137 (detail)**
Desk and bookcase, 1785–1810
Possibly Northampton County, Pennsylvania
white pine; paint; brass, bone inlay
100 1/8 × 40 3/4 × 23 5/8
Bequest of Henry Francis
du Pont 1957.0502

**Pages 138, 139 (detail)**
Tall clock, 1815
John Paul Jr. (1789–1868), Elizabethville, Dauphin County, Pennsylvania
maple, mahogany, black walnut, white pine, ash, tulip; ivory, iron, brass, painted dial
98 × 20 3/4 × 10 1/4
Bequest of Henry Francis
du Pont 1958.2874

**Page 140**
Eagle, 1865–1890
Wilhelm Schimmel (1817–1890), Cumberland Valley, Pennsylvania
white pine; paint
23 1/3 × 36 1/2 × 16
Bequest of Henry Francis
du Pont 1959.2341

**Page 141 (far left)**
Figure of a bird, 1885–1910
Attributed to "Schtockschnitzler" (cane carver) Simmons, Berks County, Pennsylvania
white pine; paint
7 1/2 × 7 × 3
Bequest of Henry Francis
du Pont 1967.0744

**(left)**
Figure of a bird, 1885–1910
Attributed to "Schtockschnitzler" (cane carver) Simmons, Berks County, Pennsylvania
white pine; paint
6 1/2 × 7 × 2 1/2
Bequest of Henry Francis
du Pont 1967.0743

**(center)**
Bird tree, 1885–1910
Attributed to "Schtockschnitzler" (cane carver) Simmons, Berks County, Pennsylvania
white pine; paint
14 × 4 1/2 × 6
Bequest of Henry Francis
du Pont 1967.0745

**(right)**
Figure of a rooster, about 1880–1938
Attributed to John Reber (1857–1938), Lehigh County, Pennsylvania
white pine; gesso and paint
7 3/8 × 6 × 3
Bequest of Henry Francis
du Pont 1967.0724.002

**Page 142**
Door lock, 1822
David Rohrer (1800–1843), Lebanon, Pennsylvania
iron, brass
7 1/8 × 9 1/2
J. Jefferson and Anne Miller
Collection 2001.0033.025

**Page 143**
Fat lamp, 1848
John Long, Lancaster County, Pennsylvania
iron, brass
10 1/4 × 3 × 4 1/2
J. Jefferson and Anne Miller
Collection 2001.0033.235

**Page 144 (left)**
Coverlet, 1834
Isaac Brubaker, New Holland, Lancaster County, Pennsylvania
wool, cotton
93 × 83
Gift of Mr. and Mrs. David
Stockwell 1968.0053

**(right)**
Quilt, 1830
Probably Bucks County, Pennsylvania
wool, cotton, silk thread
90 × 90
Museum purchase 2000.0071

**Page 146 (top)**
Cream pot, 1810 – 1860
England
earthenware
$4 \frac{5}{8} \times 4 \frac{3}{4}$
Bequest of Henry Francis
du Pont 1965.0937.001

**(middle)**
Cream pot, 1810 – 1860
England
earthenware
$3 \frac{3}{4} \times 4 \frac{1}{2}$
Bequest of Henry Francis
du Pont 1965.1228

**(bottom)**
Cream pot, 1810 – 1860
England
earthenware
$3 \frac{15}{16} \times 5 \frac{3}{16}$
Bequest of Henry Francis
du Pont 1965.1230

**Page 148 (top)**
Plate, 1800 – 1825
Pennsylvania
earthenware
$1 \frac{7}{8}$; diam: $12 \frac{1}{4}$
Gift of Henry Francis du Pont
1955.0109.005

**(bottom)**
Plate, about 1789
Attributed to George Hübener,
Montgomery County,
Pennsylvania
earthenware
$2 \frac{3}{8}$; diam: 13
Bequest of Henry Francis
du Pont 1965.2301

**Page 149**
Flowerpot, 1810 – 1840
Pennsylvania
earthenware
$8 \frac{1}{5}$; diam: 8
Bequest of Henry Francis
du Pont 1965.2313

**chapter 5**
## American Classicism

**Page 150**
Looking glass, 1800 – 1825
New York
red pine, spruce; silvered glass
$88 \frac{3}{4} \times 40 \frac{1}{2} \times 4 \frac{1}{4}$
Bequest of Henry Francis
du Pont 1957.0941

**Pages 155 (detail), 156**
*American Commissioners of the Preliminary Peace Negotiations with Great Britain*, 1783 – 1784
Benjamin West (1738 – 1820),
London
oil on canvas
$28 \frac{3}{8} \times 36 \frac{5}{16}$
Gift of Henry Francis du Pont
1957.0856

**Page 156**
Sideboard, 1795 – 1805
New York
mahogany, mahogany and satinwood veneers, light and dark wood stringing, white pine, tulip, ash; brass
$41 \frac{1}{4} \times 79 \frac{1}{2} \times 28 \frac{5}{8}$
Bequest of Henry Francis
du Pont 1957.0850

Tankards (set of six), 1772
Paul Revere (1735 – 1818), Boston
silver
$8 \frac{5}{16} \times 6 \frac{11}{16}$
Gift of Henry Francis du Pont
1957.0859.001 – .006

Candlesticks, 1759 – 1760
London
silver
$13 \times 5 \frac{9}{16} \times 5 \frac{5}{8}$
Bequest of Henry Francis du Pont
1961.0649.001 – .002a – b

Punch bowl, about 1794
Jingdezhen, China
porcelain
$6 \frac{1}{2}$; diam: 16
Gift of Henry Francis du Pont
1959.0149

Covered tureens, 1785 – 1810
Jingdezhen, China
porcelain
$6 \frac{3}{4} \times 10 \times 8 \frac{5}{8}$
Bequest of Henry Francis du Pont
1961.0647.001 – .002a – c

Urns, 1790 – 1810
Jingdezhen, China
porcelain
$16 \frac{5}{8} \times 9 \frac{3}{4}$
Bequest of Henry Francis
du Pont 1961.1041.001 – .002

Knife boxes, 1790 – 1800
England
mahogany, maple and various tropical woods inlay, deal; brass
$26 \frac{1}{2}$; diam: $11 \frac{3}{4}$
Bequest of Henry Francis
du Pont 1957.0853.001 – .002

Sconces (two of six), 1795 – 1800
Attributed to Parker and Perry,
London, England
brass; lead glass
$26 \times 12 \frac{3}{5}$
Bequest of Henry Francis
du Pont 1961.644.1 – .2

**Page 159**
Ladies desk, 1790 – 1810
Baltimore
mahogany, satinwood, mahogany and satinwood veneers, red cedar; reverse-painted glass; brass
$62 \frac{1}{8} \times 30 \frac{7}{8} \times 22 \frac{1}{4}$
Museum purchase 1957.0068

Side chair, 1790 – 1810
Baltimore
mahogany, maple, tulip, light wood inlay
$38 \frac{3}{4} \times 20 \times 20 \frac{3}{4}$
Bequest of Henry Francis
du Pont 1957.0771.001

**Page 160**
*Jerusha Benedict*, 1790
Ralph Earl (1751 – 1801),
Danbury, Connecticut
oil on canvas
$37 \frac{1}{2} \times 31 \frac{1}{2}$
Bequest of Mrs. Lammot
du Pont Copeland 2001.0049

**Page 161**
Tambour desk, 1794 – 1804
Labeled by John Seymour (1738 – 1818?) and Son (Thomas, 1771 – 1848),
Boston
mahogany, mahogany veneer, light wood inlay, white pine, white elm; brass and enamel on copper
$41 \frac{1}{2} \times 37 \frac{3}{4} \times 19 \frac{3}{4}$
Bequest of Henry Francis
du Pont 1957.0802

**Page 162**
*Mrs. Perez Morton (Sarah Wentworth Apthorp)*, 1802 – 1803
Gilbert Stuart (1755 – 1828),
Philadelphia
oil on panel
$29 \frac{1}{2} \times 24$
Gift of Henry Francis du Pont
1963.0077

**Page 163**
Plate-printed cotton, 1785 – 1790
England
cotton
$94 \frac{1}{4} \times 30 \frac{3}{4}$
Bequest of Henry Francis
du Pont 1969.3181

**Page 164**
Order of the Society of the Cincinnati badge, 1783 – 1800
Paris
gold, enamel
$1 \frac{1}{2} \times \frac{7}{8}$
Bequest of Henry Francis
du Pont 1963.0824

**Page 165**
Covered tureen, 1784
China
porcelain
$8 \frac{1}{2} \times 13 \times 9 \frac{1}{4}$
Gift of Henry Francis du Pont
1963.0700.057a – b

Platter, 1784
China
porcelain
$2 \frac{1}{16} \times 14 \frac{1}{4} \times 11 \frac{3}{4}$
Gift of Henry Francis du Pont
1963.0700.057c

Dinner plate, 1784
China
porcelain
diam: 9 9/16
Gift of Henry Francis du Pont
1963.0700.028

**Page 166**
Medal (obverse and reverse),
1789
Joseph Richardson Jr.
(1752–1831), Philadelphia
silver
5 1/2 × 4 1/8
Gift of Henry Francis du Pont
1961.1055

**Page 167**
*Washington at Verplanck's
Point*, 1790
John Trumbull (1756–1843),
New York
oil on canvas
30 × 20 1/8
Gift of Henry Francis du Pont
1964.2201

**Page 168**
*The Washington Family*,
about 1798
Edward Savage (1761–1817),
United States
oil on panel
18 1/8 × 24 1/8
Bequest of Henry Francis
du Pont 1961.0708

**Page 169**
Plate, 1795–1796
China
porcelain
1 1/8; diam: 8 1/2
Gift of Alice Braunfeld
2001.0031.001

**Page 170**
Needlework picture, 1800–1810
E. S. Sefford, United States
silk, watercolor, metallic thread;
original reverse-painted glass
and frame
15 1/4 × 16 3/4
Bequest of Henry Francis
du Pont 1957.0783

**Pages 171, 181**
Clock, 1804–1817
Jean-Baptiste Dubuc, Paris
brass, steel, glass
20 1/4 × 18 3/8 × 5 7/8
Bequest of Henry Francis
du Pont 1957.0744

**Page 173**
Armchair, 1807
Duncan Phyfe (1768–1856),
New York
mahogany, ash, cherry
33 × 21 × 23
Bequest of Henry Francis
du Pont 1957.0720.002

**Page 175**
*Victorine du Pont*, 1813
Rembrandt Peale (1778–1860),
near Wilmington, Delaware
oil on canvas
28 1/2 × 23 1/8
Bequest of Henry Francis
du Pont 1961.0709

*A series of twenty-nine
designs of modern costumes*
(London, 1823)
Henry Moses (1782?–1870)
printed by L. E. and C. M'Lean
11 × 7 3/4
Courtesy, The Winterthur Library,
Printed Book and Periodical
Collection

**Page 176**
*Klismos* side chair
(one of a pair), 1815–1825
Baltimore
tulip, maple; paint
31 3/4 × 20 1/8 × 21 1/2
Museum purchase
1992.0029.002

**Page 177**
Card table, 1800–1810
Baltimore
mahogany, white pine, tulip,
maple; paint
29 5/8 × 36 × 18 1/4
Museum purchase with partial
funds provided by an anonymous donor & Mr. and Mrs.
John R. Donnell 1999.0009

**Page 178**
Vase, 1790–1800
Josiah Wedgwood's Factory,
Staffordshire, England
stoneware (jasperware)
14 1/4; diam: 6
Museum purchase with funds
provided by Collector's Circle
and the Winterthur Centenary
Fund 1997.0014

**Page 179**
Ewer, 1812–1820
Thomas Fletcher (1787–1866)
and Sidney Gardiner
(1785–1827), Philadelphia
silver
16 × 10 5/8 × 6 3/4
Museum purchase
1969.0016

**Pages 180, 181**
Candelabra, 1810–1815
Pierre-Philippe Thomire
(1751–1843), Paris
brass, mercury gilding
22 1/4; diam: 7
Bequest of Henry Francis
du Pont 1961.1223.001

**Page 181**
Pier table, 1805–1810
Charles-Honoré Lannuier
(1779–1819), New York
mahogany and mahogany,
satinwood, and rosewood
veneers, white pine; brass
37 × 49 × 24 1/2
Bequest of Henry Francis
du Pont 1957.0685

Looking glass, 1790–1810
Albany, New York
red pine; glass; gesso, gilt
76 1/2 × 33 1/2 × 4 1/2
Bequest from the Estate of
Miss Helen DeLancey Watkins
1968.0110

**Page 182**
Illustration, from *Catalogue
of Brass Knockers, Hinges,
Escutcheons, Curtain Hooks,
Bell Pulls and Rings, Night
Bolts, Brass Ornaments,
Curtain Rods, Etc.* (possibly
Birmingham, England, 1822)
7 3/16 × 11 7/8
Courtesy, The Winterthur Library,
Printed Book and Periodical
Collection

**(top)**
Mount of river god, 1810–1830
France
gilt brass
2 3/4 × 6 1/2
Gift of Jill Ehninger Meyer
2000.0038.001

**(middle)**
Mount with swans, 1810–1830
France
gilt brass
2 1/8 × 9 3/4
Gift of Jill Ehninger Meyer
2000.0038.005a

**(bottom left)**
Escutcheon, 1810–1830
France
gilt brass
2 1/2 × 2 1/4
Gift of Jill Ehninger Meyer
2000.0038.014.002a

**(bottom right)**
Mount, 1810–1830
France
gilt brass
3 × 2
Gift of Jill Ehninger Meyer
2000.0038.006a

**Page 183**
Work table, 1817
Charles-Honoré Lannuier
(1779 – 1819), New York
mahogany, maple and rose-
wood veneers, white pine,
yellow poplar; gilded gesso,
gilded brass, die-stamped
brass borders; green baize
31 $\frac{7}{8}$ × 22 × 17 $\frac{1}{8}$
Museum purchase with funds
provided by Henry Francis du
Pont 1960.0006

**Page 184**
Coffee and tea service,
1809 – 1812
Anthony Rasch (c. 1778 – c. 1859)
and Simon Chaudron
(1758 – 1846), Philadelphia
silver; wood
Given by Mr. and Mrs. Henry
Pleasants in memory of Maria
Wilkins Smith, 1884 – 1973
1975.0080.001 – .005

**Page 185**
Sugar tongs, 1815 – 1828
Maltby Pelletreau (b. 1791),
John Bennett, and D.C.
Cooke, New York
silver
6 × 1 $\frac{1}{2}$ × 1
Museum purchase 1981.0051

**Page 186**
*Liberty Displaying the
Arts and Sciences*, about 1792
Samuel Jennings
(c. 1755 – c. 1834), Philadelphia
oil on canvas
15 × 18
Museum purchase with funds
provided by Henry Francis du
Pont 1958.0120.002

**Page 187**
*Election Day in Philadelphia*,
1815
John Lewis Krimmel
(1786 – 1821), Philadelphia
oil on canvas
16 $\frac{3}{8}$ × 25 $\frac{5}{8}$
Museum purchase with funds
provided by Henry Francis du
Pont 1959.0131

**Page 188**
Collector's cabinet, 1810 – 1820
Philadelphia
mahogany, mahogany and
satinwood veneers, tulip,
white pine; silvered glass
39 × 49 × 27
Bequest of Henry Francis
du Pont 1957.0945

## Index

*Page numbers in italics refer to photographs and captions.*

# Photography Credits

Photography by Gavin Ashworth unless otherwise noted.

Photography by Gottlieb Hampfler: Introduction, fig. 6

Photography by Bruce White: Chapter 5, fig. 28

### Introduction

Courtesy, Winterthur Museum: figs. 1, 2, 5, 6, 8, 9

Courtesy, The Winterthur Library, Winterthur Archives: fig. 3 (P101), fig. 4 (P127), fig. 7 (P46)

### Chapter 1

Courtesy, Winterthur Museum: figs. 2, 5, 17, 21

Courtesy, The Winterthur Library, Printed Book and Periodical Collection: figs. 1, 22

### Chapter 2

Courtesy, Winterthur Museum: figs. 5, 6, 7, 8, 9, 11, 16, 17, 22

Courtesy, The Winterthur Library, Printed Book and Periodical Collection: figs. 2, 10, 13

Courtesy, The Winterthur Library, Joseph Downs Collection of Manuscripts and Printed Ephemera: fig. 20 (No. 69 X 164)

### Chapter 3

Courtesy, Winterthur Museum: figs. 2, 3, 5, 6, 7, 11, 15, 22, 23, 25, 26

Courtesy, The Winterthur Library, Printed Book and Periodical Collection: figs. 10, 14

Courtesy, The Winterthur Library, Winterthur Archives: fig. 17 (P123)

### Chapter 4

Courtesy, Winterthur Museum: figs. 2, 4, 5, 10, 14, 19, 21, 25, 26

Courtesy, The Winterthur Library, Winterthur Archives: fig. 11 (P123)

### Chapter 5

Courtesy, Winterthur Museum: figs. 5, 7, 8, 12, 13, 15, 18, 31, 32

Courtesy, The Winterthur Library, Printed Book and Periodical Collection: figs. 19, 26

*For Henry Francis du Pont, 1953*

"who deserves the nobel prize for his contributions
for the preservation of American Antiquities"

Israel Sack (1883 – 1959)
antique furniture dealer, New York